'It is rare to find a book that is a true [...] midst of illness and suffering. But [...] observed book offers empathy, comp[...] [...] those who are walking the lonely and dark path that cancer often brings. Few spiritual writers can turn their own experience of suffering and depletion into something wholesome and sustaining for others. This book not only manages that but also does so with realism, authenticity, wisdom, grace and hope. This is a profound and practical book that nourishes and nurtures – soul and body alike. Gillian Straine has given us a gem to treasure.'

The Very Revd Professor Martyn Percy,
Dean of Christ Church, Oxford

'When I found out that I had cancer, I felt like I was being plunged into a different world where I didn't know the rules or how to find my way around. *Cancer: A Pilgrim Companion* offers people with cancer and those who love them a map for the journey they are about to undertake, and wisdom from a guide who has been there before them. Gillian writes with honesty and empathy from her own experience of cancer and from the healed scars it has left her with. She points us towards the death and resurrection of Jesus as the story that makes sense of what is happening to us, and that gives us hope for meaning and redemption from the pain and loss of cancer treatment. This profound book will be an anchor point for people facing a diagnosis of cancer and the people who will accompany them through it.'

Jenny Baker, author of Equals, *Chair of*
the Amos Trust and marathon runner

'In *Cancer: A Pilgrim Companion,* Gillian Straine reflects on her journey as a young woman diagnosed with a blood cancer. She does so in a way that is rich and profound. Now ordained, Gillian weaves together a narrative of theological, biblical and liturgical depth earthed in human experience and the story of God in Christ. I can see this book being of great help to those who are making – or have made – such a journey for themselves or shared it with a loved one.'

The Rt Revd Lee Rayfield, Bishop of Swindon

'Gillian Straine has produced a deeply personal and searingly honest theological reflection on her own experience of joining what she calls the "cancer community". While tackling major themes such as "meaning" and "vulnerability", she explores the "gift of cancer" – which is the way in which it exposes the myth that we are truly in control of our own lives. Her recurring emphasis on the importance of relationship and her use of pilgrimage as a metaphor for her own journey makes this a valuable and readable book of practical guidance and encouragement for fellow travellers. The message is clear and simple: God is with us, and there is hope.'

The Rt Revd James Newcome, Bishop of Carlisle and the Church of England's lead bishop on health

The Revd Dr Gillian Straine is Director of the Guild of Health and St Raphael. An Anglican priest, she also has a doctorate in physics from Imperial College London and is the author of *Introducing Science and Religion: A path through polemic* (SPCK, 2014). Gillian was diagnosed with cancer at the age of 21 and has been in remission since 2002. She lives in London with her husband and two young children.

CANCER

A pilgrim companion

GILLIAN STRAINE

First published in Great Britain in 2017

Society for Promoting Christian Knowledge
36 Causton Street
London SW1P 4ST
www.spck.org.uk

*This book is dedicated to Jeff Horn and all the staff at
the Haematology Unit, Aberdeen Royal Infirmary*

Ad maiorem Dei gloriam

Contents

Acknowledgements

There are many people from all areas of my life whom I must thank for helping me with the production of this book. I would like to begin by thanking SPCK for giving me the opportunity to write it. My editor, Tracey Messenger, has been an invaluable source of encouragement and patience in this project.

The origin of the book lies in a shock diagnosis of cancer in 2000, when my life seriously deviated from my expectations and plans. Later, when I was training for the Anglican priesthood, I was able to spend time thinking, reading and revisiting my experience, chiefly in preparation for a pastoral ministry among the ill, dying and grief-stricken. Therefore I am extremely grateful for the latitude that Martyn Percy, the principal of Ripon College Cuddesdon, afforded me in the pursuit of this study, and for the support of my tutor Margaret Whipp.

Many people have taken the time to listen to my ideas and discuss their theological implications; they include John Swinton at Aberdeen University, David Wilkinson at St John's College, Durham and colleagues in the Science and Religion Forum, in particular Mark Harris and Michael Fuller, both of Edinburgh University.

Many people and their stories have influenced my thinking about cancer and have been part of my own journey through the experience of both treatment and remission. I have been privileged to be alongside many people with cancer – in particular, Stephanie Williamson, Marina Sotiriou, Katharine Waldrum, David and Meg Heywood, and my friends at the Guild of Health and St Raphael – and to listen to their stories, which have formed the foundation of this book and provided the inspiration for its writing.

This book is a product of my own journey through cancer, and so I would like to pay tribute to those who travelled with me and helped me find a way out of the wilderness. They include the doctors and nurses at Aberdeen Royal Infirmary, in particular my consultant Mr C. and my chemotherapy nurse, Jeff Horn, and my friends who came alongside me when I was ill and recovering: Easter Smart, Julianne Smith, Tara and Jamie McDonald-Gibson and Paul Miller. And thanks to Philomena O'Hara who listened. I would also like to thank Tim Goode and Stephanie Williamson, who read and commented on the early drafts of the book, and my wonderful in-laws Rosslie and Stephen Platten, who also took the time to proofread and comment, not to mention looking after the grandchildren.

It doesn't seem enough to simply thank my parents, Ron and Kathleen, for their love and care when I was ill. Words cannot begin to do justice to what you did for me. I will never know what you went through and I only hope that I can be half as good a parent to my sons as you are to me. Thank you.

Finally, I thank my husband Gregory for his endless encouragement and support as this book took me back to some difficult places from which I occasionally needed rescuing. Thank you for making me laugh, for supporting me and for putting up with me.

A beginning

All cancer journeys have a beginning. Normally, a beginning is a positive moment, one where a new start is made and there are plans and dreams and hopes. A beginning conjures up images of the first green buds of spring, or an adventurer setting out on a new expedition. A beginning contains new possibilities. But the beginning of a cancer journey is quite different.

There is usually a place in time and space that can be identified as *the moment*, the instant when and where it all began. The journey through cancer might be one that you are taking yourself, or one that you are taking as you accompany a family member or friend who has the disease. As a pastor, you might be stepping in and out of the cancer journeys of your flock, and journeying with them in prayer as part of a network of care. Whatever the circumstances of the journey it will have had that beginning.

Perhaps it began in a stab of worry that sent you to your doctor. Or it was the unexpected late night telephone call, or the nervously expected and dreaded call from the hospital, too soon to be good news. Perhaps it was the moment when the doctor said, 'I'm sorry, but . . .' Perhaps it was when you told your child, or parent, or partner 'the news'. Perhaps it was when you cried for the first time, or held someone else as they cried. Whenever and wherever that moment happened, that was the beginning of your cancer journey, one you had no choice but to begin.

The beginning of a cancer journey is unlike any other beginning that you might have made. It is impossible to underplay the dizzying effects, the initial confusion and disorientation. All your plans for the future come under scrutiny in the light of a diagnosis of cancer. The firm foundations of life and the hoped-for future are shaken and made unstable by the illness. Other previously important concerns pale into insignificance as the mass of cancer parks itself firmly on top of us. It appears to change everything, and it seems as if its gravitational pull distorts all aspects of our life's trajectory, creating chaos everywhere – in our relationships, work, finances and happiness. There is nothing that cancer doesn't affect as it squashes life and clouds the horizon.

The weight of cancer is the fear that it stirs up. Fear of the future, fear of the treatment. What will it do to my body? How will I cope? How will everyone else cope? When will I be back to 'normal'? And these fears cascade out, affecting all those whose own lives orbit the one with the disease. The fear that cancer causes is the ultimate fear, the mortal threat under which we all live, brought nearer and into sharp focus by a disease that has blundered into our life uninvited.

As the cancer diagnosis hurtles around your life it may initially produce all sorts of damage. It breaks down order and disturbs your foundations. It casts dark clouds over your future plans so that it may seem hard to see clearly ahead any more. Previously sunny skies are replaced by clouds, and rumbling away is the thunder of rightful anger and honest grief at what has been lost. As the burden is shouldered and carried out to be shared with loved ones, the effects of cancer ripple into the community that surrounds the one who has been diagnosed, washing up on some quite unexpected shores, and bringing to bear on the person who is ill in both positive and negative ways.

This is the beginning of the cancer journey, an expedition defined by loss, uncertainty and fear. But it is only the beginning. There is a journey to be made, a difficult journey undeniably, but it is your journey. It is your path to tread and yours to define despite its unwanted incursion into your life. Unashamedly, and wisely, it is to our faith that we particularly turn when we are facing hard times and difficult journeys.

The Christian faith has often been understood as a journey or a pilgrimage on earth to heaven, one in which the faithful seek in the travelling to understand the divine and then use this knowledge to influence how we live. Looking back through the history of people who have thought about God, we can see a constant tug of war among theologians between ideas of the 'up-there-in-heaven'

Creator God, knowing all and all-powerful, and the 'down-here-on-earth' God, seen particularly through Jesus. So it is too for the individual Christian who seeks to find a balance between the Creator of the universe and Jesus who joined us on earth, loving and laughing, suffering and dying. Working this out is as much the job of the theologian as it is for us who balance our complicated lives, believing or even merely suspecting that the life of faith taps into something more powerful than we can put into words, however clever.

The Gospel accounts of Jesus' life have been used for centuries as places where human beings can understand not only Jesus and God, but also our own lives. We see Jesus alone and abandoned in the Garden of Gethsemane asking God to take away the cup, asking for his future to be different. We read of Jesus' suffering on the cross, demanding to know why God seems to have abandoned him. And we have the eyewitness accounts of perhaps the strangest event in human history, the resurrection of Christ, with his curiously unrecognizable body. The threefold journey, also called the Paschal journey, is the focus of Holy Week and Easter, but it is also more widely a place of reflection as we seek to understand our own lives, and particularly our suffering, in the light of faith.

One of the greatest gifts of the Christian faith is its explanation of suffering, and its attempts to answer the haunting question: if God loves us, why does he allow us to suffer? For me, the question is answered through accompaniment. We are not simply flung a few theological answers to ponder; nor are we invited to see suffering as a test, or this life merely as a 'vale of soul making'. The answer is the offer of a companion, a fellow sufferer. For God sent his only Son Jesus Christ, so that all who live and believe in him will never be left alone in their suffering. Our sufferings have been taken into the heart of God through Christ, and it is to his life that we may turn to understand our own sufferings, our journeys into places that we do not wish to go.

This book is designed as a companion on your cancer journey. Its threefold sequence of diagnosis, treatment and outcome mirrors Jesus' own journey from the Garden of Gethsemane, through the cross, to the resurrection. In each phase, we shall consider the physical, psychological and social burdens of the disease, and draw on the wisdom of Christian faith to find solace, encouragement and direction.

I shall draw on my own experience of cancer, both treatment and recovery, and my experience that deep meaning is to be found on the pilgrimage through cancer. As an Anglican priest, I have accompanied many people on their cancer journey and have seen the power of the journeying metaphor and the extraordinary hope and grace that flourish even in the darkest of places when stories of suffering are told. The cancer journey took me somewhere I did not want to go, but it was also a journey that allowed me to glimpse the resurrection truth that suffering does not destroy. Indeed when Easter Day dawned on my remission I was able to see that all was not loss, but that glimmers of new creation and possibility gave meaning to my experience of cancer. For the risen Christ confirms the unexpected, that even a body with scars and a head full of worries about relapse gives rise to God's delight, and is given a mission in this beautiful and fragile world. That is the hope on which this book is founded.

Whether you are on the journey yourself, or are walking alongside someone as a companion, as a Christian you have the possibility of inviting Christ along on the journey. And so the cancer journey, though frightening, becomes a little less lonely; it can begin more like the beginnings we are used to, full of plans and dreams and hopes.

Matthew's account of Jesus' journey is bookended by a key thought given to those who accompanied him. In Matthew 1, the angel of the Lord appears to Joseph in a dream and tells him not to be afraid, for the birth of Jesus has been foretold by the prophet: '"Look, the virgin shall conceive and bear a son, and they shall name him Emmanuel", which means, "God is with us"' (Matthew 1.23). And then in the final chapter of the Gospel, we hear the echo from the beginning: the angel greets the women at the empty tomb and says 'Do not be afraid' (Matthew 28.10). Jesus' journey was encircled by the command not to be afraid; it is a message that we are wise to pack in our bags as we begin our own journey, comforted by the final words of the Gospel of Matthew, offered by the risen Christ: 'And remember, I am with you always' (Matthew 28.20).

For we do not journey alone, but with the One who saves us, who bears our souls for us, and whose Spirit prays within us. This knowledge can never take away all fear and doubt, but it frames our journey. God is with us. This is the faith. Even when we are in pain, fearful, anxious, doubting or angry, God is with us on the journey ahead, leading and lighting the way. So let us begin our journey together, with courage to face whatever comes, knowing that we are always surrounded by God's love and light, no matter how dark it gets.

MY LORD GOD, I have no idea where I am going. I do not see the road ahead of me. I cannot know for certain where it will end. Nor do I really know myself, and the fact that I think I am following your will does not mean that I am actually doing so. But I believe that the desire to please you does in fact please you. And I hope I have that desire in all that I am doing. I hope that I will never do anything apart from that desire. And I know that if I do this you will lead me by the right road, though I may know nothing about it. Therefore I will trust you always though I may seem to be lost and in the shadow of death. I will not fear, for you are ever with me, and you will never leave me to face my perils alone.   *Thomas Merton*[1]

1

The landscape

Who would true valour see,
Let him come hither;
One here will constant be,
Come wind, come weather.
There's no discouragement
Shall make him once relent
His first avowed intent
To be a pilgrim.

John Bunyan, The Pilgrim's Progress

O Lord, you have searched me and known me.

Psalm 139.1

The Lord went in front of them in a pillar of cloud by day,
to lead them along the way, and in a pillar of fire by night,
to give them light, so that they might travel by day and by
night.

Exodus 13.21

Your word is a lamp to my feet
and a light to my path.

Psalm 119.105

For I am convinced that neither death, nor life, nor angels,
nor rulers, nor things present, nor things to come, nor
powers, nor height, nor depth, nor anything else in all
creation, will be able to separate us from the love of God
in Christ Jesus our Lord.

Romans 8.39

Introduction

Cancer is often described as a journey and, as with all journeys, before setting out it is important to know as much as possible about what lies ahead. If the journey was, for example, a hike in the mountains, we would first plan our route and try to gather information about what it might entail. We would need to pack for our expedition, and remember a map and a compass to guide us, a torch in case we got lost and some extra food to keep our energy levels up. We would check the weather, and ensure that we had the skills to face what lay ahead. We might also take advice and talk to those who had followed the route before us. And finally, as all good mountaineers know, we would tell others where we were going and might even invite along a friend to travel with us. In this chapter we shall pack our bag for the journey through cancer, hoping that in doing some preparation we might be a little more ready for the challenges which lie ahead.

The journey that we are about to begin is not one that we have chosen and our destination is unknown. But it is an expedition nevertheless, one that will take us into a strange world, and it is a journey that has the potential to change us. For we may not have chosen to embark upon it, but we do have choices about how the roads ahead are navigated. This book offers guidance to transforming the journey which begins with a cancer diagnosis into a pilgrimage into the knowledge and love of God.

The English term 'pilgrim' is derived from the Latin word *peregrinum*, meaning a foreigner, a stranger, someone on a journey or a temporary resident. The idea of pilgrimage is part of most world faiths; for example the Haj pilgrimage, an important element of the Islamic faith, or the Christian journey to the shrine of St James the Great in Santiago de Compostela; it appears to be a feature of human nature to desire what pilgrimage can bring. In the Judeo-Christian tradition, pilgrimage links to the call of Abram by God to take his family on a journey into a strange place to find the Promised Land (Genesis 12.1ff).

The word 'pilgrimage' is used to mean so much more than a simple journey from A to B, or a means of transport to a special place. It is a way of travelling that is both physical and spiritual, where the journey is not a tourist holiday but rather an age-old route into the knowledge of God. It is a real journey, for example to Jerusalem or Rome, but made with a spiritual goal and with the intention of drawing closer to God, expecting transformation and deepening knowledge along the way. To be a pilgrim is not a means to an end, but a way of travelling with a heightened expectation of drawing closer to God.

The expectation on the journey through cancer, as on any pilgrimage, is to find the pearl of great price – to discover the meaning in the experience. Viktor Frankl, the Austrian psychiatrist and Holocaust survivor, wrote, 'Man is not destroyed by suffering; he is destroyed by suffering without meaning.'[1] The significance will be unique to each of us who makes this type of journey; we set out knowing that we will be challenged and possibly even changed, but with a confidence based on the knowledge that God will never leave us.

On our journey we will encounter medical tests, waiting rooms, physical discomfort, fear and pain. The journey might involve operating tables and there is going to be a lot of waiting around. We are going to new places and we will meet new people. There will be highs and lows, and we will sometimes have to be carried by others. We may also occasionally have to support the people around us. There will be the shockingly unexpected and the gut-wrenchingly mundane. We are going to have to pack well.

The first thing we shall pack into our hypothetical bag is some knowledge. The phrase 'knowledge is power' is commonly attributed to the philosopher and scientist Francis Bacon (1561–1626), and, as Bacon is frequently seen as the father of the scientific method, let's pack some science about cancer. Cancer is an ancient disease, originating in the genetic code that makes each of us unique, and today its study is an enormous industry. Understanding a little of what cancer is in biochemical terms empowers us both clinically and as human individuals to understand what is happening to our bodies.

Cancer seems particularly vulnerable to powerful rumour, myth and taboo. We will examine where these myths originate and then examine why it is best to leave them behind. We do not need to carry dead weight and issues that will only slow us down. Science will help us to critique the taboo of cancer, keeping our feet firmly in the reality of our situation and giving us power through knowledge.

However, cancer is more than just biochemistry: it is a disease that begins a cascade of changes. Our daily routine and work life may change; we might look different, and it might change how others see us. Cancer has a fundamental impact on human identity. Those with cancer have left behind the 'silence of health'[2] and have had unwillingly to enter the clamour of the hospital waiting room and the discord of an uncertain future. And so into our bag we shall also pack some clear ideas about what makes us human, so that we are prepared on the journey ahead to understand how cancer can alter aspects of our identity.

As we pack in the knowledge, leave out the taboo, consider our identity and invite in companions, we do so as pilgrims knowing that Christ is with us. Our spiritual tradition forms a key component of our identity and in the final section of this chapter we will consider how the journey ahead is affected by our faith, asking how this changes the paths we take and the ground that we will cover.

The psalmist reminds us that there is nowhere we can go that escapes the love of God:

> Where can I go from your spirit? Or where can I flee from your presence? . . . If I take the wings of the morning and settle at the farthest limits of the sea, even there your hand shall lead me, and your right hand shall hold me fast.
>
> *Psalm 139.7, 9–10*

Our identity is entirely known, and is loved by God: 'For it was you who formed my inward parts; you knit me together in my mother's womb' (Psalm 139.13).

Pilgrimage is a journey into the knowledge and love of God, and as we make our pilgrim way through the land of cancer we ponder it all in the light of faith, and ask to find the meaning for us in the experience. But we do so with confidence and peace, for there is no place, no self-discovery, no science that can separate us from God (Romans 8.38–39) – so let's get packing!

Cancer: history, histology and pathology

Cancer has existed for as long as there have been human beings. The earliest written record of cancer is in the Egyptian Edwin Smith Papyrus, dating from 1600 BCE, which seems to refer to a cancer of the breast. The origin of the word 'cancer' comes from the Greek physician Hippocrates (*ca.* 460–370 BCE), who used the terms *carcinos* and *carcinoma* to describe tumours. These words are derived from the Greek word for 'crab', chosen because the shapes of tumours, with their finger-like projections, are reminiscent of the legs and pincers of the sea creature. A later scholar, Galen (*ca.* AD 130–200), used the word *oncos*, meaning 'swelling', to describe tumours, and from this comes oncology, the medical name for the study of cancer.

In the eighteenth century, connections were first made between the disease and possible external causes. In 1761, the English physician John Hill (1716–75) made a connection between tobacco snuff and nose cancer. And in 1775 Sir Percival Potts (1714–88) wrote about scrotal cancers of men who had previously worked as chimney sweeps. In the nineteenth century the study of cancer was accelerated by the invention of the modern microscope, not only in terms of deepening knowledge but in the variety of treatments that were developed as a result.

The modern field of oncology is largely dominated by genetic science, which has its roots in the pioneering work of the Augustinian friar Gregor Mendel (1822–84). In the present day, the study of oncology has been vastly boosted by the completion in 2003 of the human genome project, which mapped the sequence of human DNA.[3] Today, billions are spent globally on researching cancer, its causes and treatments.

So, what exactly is cancer? Simply put, cancer is a disease which involves uncontrolled cell multiplication. This activity is not itself the problem; indeed all life depends on the ability of a single cell to reproduce. Problems only occur when cellular replication is uninhibited and happens to the detriment of the body as a whole.

You may think that your body is a static object that ages with you, but most of the cells in your body have a short life cycle. For example, cells in the small intestine are renewed every two to four days,[4] while red blood cells are on about a four-month cycle.[5] In the normal pattern of healthy life and growth a cell will develop, divide and then die when it is old or damaged in some way. When a cell divides into two daughter cells, the genetic material it contains is copied and carried into the two duplicate cells. Normally this proceeds without error, and each succeeding generation is genetically identical to those that came before. It is an ongoing process involving nearly all the trillion or so cells in your body, working in harmony and delicately observing one another.

Cancer is the name given to a group of diseases which emerge at the genetic level when something goes wrong in the process of cell division. An error allows cells to multiply without any control, and/or not to die when they should. This uncontrolled division may form lumps of cells, which are called tumours.

Cancer begins with a single cell that 'decides' to do its own thing, without consideration of the greater organism. This type of 'self-interested' biochemistry is a surprisingly unlikely event, given all the cell division that goes on in a human body over its lifetime. But when it does happen, when one cell begins rapid and uncontrolled multiplication, the eventual effect is serious.

> The cancer cell is a renegade. Unlike their normal counter-parts, cancer cells disregard the needs of the community of cells around them. Cancer cells are only interested in their own proliferative advantage. They are selfish and very unsociable. Most important, unlike normal cells, they have learned to grow without any prompting from the community of cells around them.[6]

As cancer grows, it may influence the surrounding tissues, for example forming cells that allow blood to flow to the tumour and for waste products to be taken away. Not all tumours are cancerous. Benign tumours can grow in the body and remain isolated in one area. Cancerous tumours on the other hand are malignant, meaning that the cancer cells can spread into other tissues, or travel around the body and begin a new tumour at a different site (this is called *metastasis*).

Cancer can begin almost anywhere in the body. Indeed, there are more than 100 types of cancer, usually named after the organ in which they begin, for example lung cancer. There are exceptions to this, such as leukaemia, which begins where blood is formed in the bones and doesn't lead to the growth of tumours but instead to the development of large numbers of abnormal white blood cells.

Given its origin in uncontrolled multiplication and its undermining of the handbrake mechanisms which exist to prevent such multiplication, it is perhaps easy to think of cancer as an enraged bull, hurtling around the body, causing damage and taking control by sheer force. But the biochemistry reveals something a great deal more subtle. Cancer is more like a skilful, wily fox tricking cells into compliance and subverting the systems designed to prevent it getting its claws into the body's well-defended functions. This can be seen most clearly when we examine why cancerous growth begins in the first place.

The root of all cancer lies in the 'blueprint' of the cell, the genetic information that regulates how a cell grows and divides. Certain genes, sometimes called the 'drivers', tend to contribute to cancer:

- *Proto oncogenes* These are parts of a cell's genetic code linked to reproduction and growth, and they are susceptible to becoming oncogenes through mutations of the code. The oncogenes are sometimes called the 'cancer genes' and are responsible for cancer-like cell division.
- *Tumour suppressor genes* These act as checks and balances to the system, stopping runaway growth. However, if cancer deactivates these genes then uncontrolled growth will be allowed.
- *DNA repair genes* As the name suggests, these fix damaged parts of the genetic code, but if mutations occur in them, errors will appear in other genes and together this can cause cancer.

Normally, changes in many genes are required for cancer to begin. But next we must address why these mutations to the genetic code happen in the first place.

First, it might be down to random mutations. Given the sheer volume of cellular multiplication in the body, there is a chance of errors occurring which may lead to the development of cancer. Second, there are environmental factors that might damage a gene and cause a mutation. These include radiation, tobacco smoke, diet, obesity and infections. There are also a small number of cancers which have a hereditary element, such as breast cancer and the associated BRCA1 and BRCA2 gene. Most cancers have multiple causes and it is often hard to isolate a single cause in any individual. It is a matter of ongoing research as to which factor has the upper hand, but it can be said that all cancers are caused by a combination of 'bad luck' (the random mutation), the environment and heredity.[7]

But even once a mutation occurs, the cancer operates genetically to protect its own survival. One of the cleverest tricks of the cancer attack is to undermine a cell's natural clock and its own suicide programme. Cellular DNA has an ingenious way of remembering how many times it has already reproduced in order to safeguard against eternal multiplication. DNA stores information in a string of code made of biochemical compounds called bases. At both ends of the DNA structure, there are particular sequences of bases called telomeres. After each replication the telomeres are shortened by about 100 bases. When the ends of the telomeres are reached, the cells will stop replicating. Some cancer cells however manage to 'resurrect' the enzyme which can remake the telomeres, thus subverting a natural way to stop cell division.

A cell also has its own self-destruct programme called *cell apoptosis*. A cell may activate this rapid death for any of several reasons, including during the development of the embryo, in the immune system during the production of the correct antibodies, if the cell's DNA is damaged or if the cell receives a biochemical signal from its own regulatory mechanisms that it is not growing correctly. The latter may be raised in the event that a cancer cell is detected. In addition, all cells will activate their suicide programme if an oncogene is activated. It seems like a failsafe security system. But this too the cancer has wheedled out of, cleverly circumnavigating cell apoptosis in several ways, including through a gene mutation, particularly the tumour suppressor gene known as p53.

The biochemistry is fascinating; it reveals an extraordinary world of cellular function, balance, beauty and complexity. And it goes without saying that what we are dealing with is more than simply interesting science: this is a disease that kills, and will have a direct impact on one in two people in the UK in their lifetime.[8]

But the science of cancer is clear in one respect: cancer is *not* the bogeyman, nor is it punishment for bad behaviour. The science shows that cancer is *morally neutral*. It is almost as if cancer needs to be rebranded: 'Cancer: it's not personal, it's biochemistry.' But that is not always easy to remember, as we will explore in the next section.

The cancer taboo

I was aware of the taboo surrounding cancer before I ever read about it. It is easy to spot it on TV adverts and in media headlines and, if you are living with a cancer diagnosis, it makes its presence very well known. I remember being in a large group of people on a rare night out when I was ill. Someone I didn't know asked me what I did (and how we like to identify each other through our utility!), and cried when I said I didn't *do* anything because I was being treated for cancer. Suddenly, part of your life is not suitable for mentioning in polite company. 'Cancer' flags up images of bald-headed children and pain-racked bodies, the death of maiden aunts and beloved grannies. Indeed, mention the c-word and you will be greeted with silence, as the song evocatively puts it.[9]

Sometimes people won't even say the word, preferring instead 'lump', or 'tumour', or 'growth'. What to call the disease probably first becomes an issue when you have received the diagnosis and have to tell other people. Is it best just to blunder in and say it? Or is it better to break the news gently with a suitable euphemism and then brace yourself for whatever reaction you are presented with? It is a brave conversationalist who attempts to drop it casually into a chat, for it is a word that summons up ghouls and terror, seemingly beyond its biological power and certainly beyond the danger that it poses today given the advances in medicine. Yet doctors would far rather give a diagnosis of heart disease, despite it typically being more dangerous than cancer; such is the power of the taboo, for cancer is regularly named as the most feared disease in the UK.[10]

And it is not just in conversation that cancer is unwelcome; cancer is very seldom the topic of art, poetry and literature. Indeed, illness as a whole is seen as universally not worth such endeavours, as Virginia Woolf humorously pointed out:

> Considering how common illness is, how tremendous the spiritual change that it brings, how astonishing, when the lights of health go down, the undiscovered countries that are then disclosed, what wastes and deserts of the soul a slight attack of influenza brings to light ... it becomes strange indeed that illness has not taken its place with love, battle, and jealousy among the prime themes of literature. Novels, one would have thought, would have been devoted to influenza; epic poems to typhoid; odes to pneumonia, lyrics to toothache. But no ... literature does its best to maintain that its concern is with the mind; that the body is a sheet of plain glass through which the soul looks straight and clear.[11]

People typically use language heavily laden with war images to describe the experience. Harold Pinter (1930–2008) described his cancer as a battle in the poem 'Cancer Cells', written in 2002 when he was having chemotherapy.[12] It is a rather sinister portrayal of his fight with his tumour, personified as being intent on his death.

'Cancer cells are those which have forgotten how
to die' – nurse, Royal Marsden hospital

They have forgotten how to die
And so extend their killing life.

I and my tumour dearly fight.
Let's hope a double death is out.

I need to see my tumour dead
A tumour which forgets to die
But plans to murder me instead.

But I remember how to die
Though all my witnesses are dead.

But I remember what they said
Of tumours which would render them
As blind and dumb as they had been
Before the birth of that disease
Which brought the tumour into play.

The black cells will dry up and die
Or sing with joy and have their way.
They breed so quietly night and day,
You never know, they never say.

Pinter understands his treatment to be a 'fight' against an insidious enemy and his choice of words is very reminiscent of much language used almost casually in relation to cancer. How often do we say or hear 'She is fighting bravely' or 'He has lost his battle'? Indeed, avoiding the use of such language and images is actually quite difficult.

The military metaphor for illness has a long history. John Donne (1572–1631) wrote in his *Devotions upon Emergent Occasions* that his illness was like a siege within his body: 'The disease hath established a kingdom, an empire in me, and will have certain *arcana imperii*, secrets of state, by which it will proceed and not be bound to declare them.'[13]

The military metaphor does in some ways reflect what happens once cancer has appeared in the body, taking it over by force and seeking new territory (metastasis). St Jerome, in one of the earliest records of cancer, puts it succinctly, observing: 'The one there with his swollen belly is pregnant with his own death.'

People have talked about waging a war on cancer since the 1970s, when Richard Nixon and Ted Kennedy began to throw serious money into oncological research.[14] The military metaphor for cancer has appeal outside the clinical setting. When, for example, an organization is said to be cancerous, it means that there is something within which is bad or evil, taking it over from the inside. John Dean explained to Richard Nixon about Watergate: 'We have a cancer within, close to the presidency – that's growing.'[15]

The Italian Renaissance scholar Petrarch noted that 'Suspicion is the cancer of friendship'; and Theodore Roosevelt used the following words as he addressed the Workingmen's Red Cross

Sunday Celebration, as reproduced in the *New York Times* of 1 October 1917: 'Germany has reduced savagery to a science, and this great war for the victorious peace of justice must go on until the German cancer is cut clean out of the world body.'

Some will naturally be attracted by the metaphor, for fighting to win something is not an alien concept. Indeed, fighting is very much part of what it means to be human in an evolutionary sense:

> Anything's possible. You can be told you have a 90-percent chance or a 50-percent chance or a 1-percent chance, but you have to believe, and you have to fight. By fight I mean arm yourself with all the available information, get second opinions, third opinions, fourth opinions. Understand what has invaded your body, and what the possible cures are.[16]

When I was ill, I was frequently subject to the military metaphor for cancer: Be brave, soldier on, fight hard, be strong. Yet while such words were always meant sincerely and as nothing but encouragement, I felt uneasy about them: they made me feel belittled, disempowered, even scared. I knew that I had done nothing to deserve this illness, and that it was probably the result of random mutations or an inherited susceptibility. And I also knew that no matter how hard I tried, or how bravely I endured treatment, they might not work and I might die. What then for these comforting metaphors?

John Diamond, in his book *C: Because Cowards Get Cancer Too . . .* , describes the problem with the military metaphor for cancer well. He particularly attacks the idea of bravery in association with the cancer patient. He points out that when one describes a cancer patient as brave then the definition of bravery itself has been changed. Bravery usually involves an element of choice. One is brave because one decides to risk one's own life and dash into a burning building to save someone. Unhelpfully, being brave has been reduced to enduring any kind of suffering. He writes, heartbreakingly, 'The five year old leukaemia victim is always "brave little Linda" . . . What is it not to be brave though? Which is the cowardly five year old leukaemic? The one who scrawls a crayoned message saying she can't go on like this and tops herself?'[17]

Metaphors are useful ways of helping us to understand complex situations but they can also lead to stigma and stereotypes. Furthermore, metaphors may be great in general, but when applied to individuals they may have very personal resonances. For me, I was repelled by any military metaphor being applied to the cancer within my body or my own response to it, or to the treatments I was given. One of the problems with the military metaphor is that it reflects male dominance models in medicine and ideas of medical authoritarianism.[18] It can maintain the position of the patient as passive and uninvolved compared to the doctor who wields the scalpel, or prescribes the weapons of war, whether chemical or radiation. Nor could I accept the idea, however encouraging it was meant to be, that if I fought hard enough I would beat it. I was going to do my best to survive, but I knew that in the end that was no guarantee of survival. I didn't like the military metaphor because I didn't believe in it.

I am going to beat this, I will win. You will be OK because you will fight it hard. This rhetoric carries some dark corollaries. If one does not win, was it because the battle had not been fought hard or nobly enough? A recent cancer fund advertising for money for much-needed research used the slogan 'I shouldn't be here'. Obviously they wished to show that the money they received would be used to research new treatments so that more people could survive the disease. But I couldn't help asking, as a 'survivor' of the cancer battle – why shouldn't I be here?

Statistics have a similar effect when we are considering cancer and should be used with care around those who are ill. A survival rate of 80 per cent may sound encouraging; indeed, those would be rather good odds if they were applied to a horse race. But I found that they were of little comfort and did not answer all my doubts and fears: someone had to be in the other 20 per cent, and why should it not be me? The mathematics of cancer may be of comfort to some – indeed they may be of great interest too – but they will never be the great sop for all fear and anxiety, at least not until we have a survival rate of 100 per cent.

In confronting the taboo of cancer, and indeed gaining control of the journey which lies ahead, it is vitally important to find

words, images and metaphors that work for the one who is tread-
ing across the land of cancer. People have often used 'journey' – as
have I in this book – as an alternative metaphor for the experience
of cancer; others have preferred 'rollercoaster'. Yet others have
suggested that an ecological metaphor might be more useful.[19]
Such a metaphor summons up ideas like balance, sustainability,
natural, quality of life, diversity, renewable, community and con-
servation. In an ecological metaphor health would take into
account the natural limits of life, and concentrate on improving
quality of life.

A poem by the American poet Philip Appleman illustrates the
medical and military aspects of cancer in comparison to how the
protagonist saw his own disease as very much part of himself and
of nature. The cancer in 'Uncle Jimmie' is described as being like
a rat gnawing away at his face, an infestation in his own body,
a disgusting vermin. But he also sees the disease as part of the
natural world:

> Uncle Jimmie had a hunch that cancer,
> the rat that gnawed away behind his ears,
> was part of the warm earth and silver woods
> and snowy meadows in the mountains.

Modern medicine is intent on curing him by cutting out more
and more of his face. And those of faith, underestimating the
importance of the body, want Jimmie to pray and to believe more
in his soul than his body. Neither is able to see his cancer as Jimmie
does:

> But the rat kept gnawing, and Auntie Flo went on
> reading St. Paul (The works of the flesh are uncleanness),
> and praying, and paying the bills – and the surgeons huddled,
> frowning at Jimmie's want of reverence
> for faith and modern medicine.

In the end the rat is completely cut out of Jimmie. He is technic-
ally still alive, but he is left with a shattered life. He can no
longer speak, nor see, nor, in the end, even remember who he
once was.

Auntie Flo comes every day
to read to bandages the Word Made Flesh,
and pray, and pay the bills, and watch with Jimmie,
whittled down like a dry stick, but living:
the heart, in its maze of tubes, pumps on,
while catbirds mock the calling of cardinals,
artichokes grow dusty green in sunshine,
butterflies dally with the roses,
and Uncle Jimmie is no part of these.

The tragedy of this life is not that Uncle Jimmie gets cancer, but that neither medicine nor faith understand the meaning of life or the place of death.

Part of the healing of the cancer taboos will come about as the treatments become more successful and produce fewer side effects. Perhaps as treatments shift from the harsh sledgehammers of chemotherapy and radiotherapy to other treatments such as gene therapy, the military metaphors will lose their prominence.

All metaphors of the experience of cancer betray their underlying understandings of death. For the military metaphor the danger lies in the implication that death is the result of failure. In contrast, metaphors which emphasize the experience as part of a journey or as part of the natural world see death not as loss but as an integral part of the created order. That is why I have chosen the metaphor of journey or pilgrimage for this book.

But the taboo about cancer goes deeper than the military metaphors. Cancer is more than the clinical disease, the actual suffering of patients and those who love them and the justifiable fear of that suffering. The social reality of the disease, in a way that mirrors its physicality, may take on an independent life of its own. Cancer is the fearful monster of folklore, the Grendel of *Beowulf*, which comes in the dark to make manifest your worst fears.

In 1978 Susan Sontag wrote about this subject in her work *Illness as Metaphor*.[20] Here she expands on both tuberculosis and cancer as diseases 'encumbered by metaphors' and demonized by taboo. In 1988 the work was extended as she looked at AIDS from the same vantage point.

Sontag describes the popular understanding of cancer as an 'obscene' disease or an ill omen; it is abominable, repugnant, a disgrace. In its own mythology, cancer is a disease which corrodes from the inside. It causes its victims to lose their appetite for life, for both food and sex. Indeed, they become listless and tired and, as a result of treatment, they lose their hair and become desexualized. It is a slow disease, causing those it infests to lose all passion and to shrivel up. But more than this, cancer itself is a malevolent life force, an alien spreading around the body and consuming the victim from the inside. As the disease progresses, the identity of the victim is sucked away in pain so at the last the disease triumphs over the individual. Very few deaths from cancer have been popularly portrayed as noble. Sontag drew out the idea of cancer as taboo, and although it is uncomfortable to think about cancer in such a way, her approach gets close to the root of why cancer is so much more than just a clinical diagnosis.

If death from cancer is mythologically the subject of taboo, then the causes of the disease too may be held up for judgement. Cancer is generally held to be a Western disease, and thus a symptom of a decadent and greedy lifestyle. And so cancer is itself a moral judgement.

There is a long history of the link between health and emotions, and out of it the 'cancer personality' has been born. This is the idea that certain personalities or emotional predispositions lead to the growth of tumours. Galen in the second century noted that melancholic women were more likely to get breast cancer. Sir Astley Cooper (1768–1841), the English surgeon and anatomist, wrote that grief and anxiety were the most famous causes of breast cancer.

At times in the past, cancer was thought to be a moralistic disease in which the body turned against itself, taken over from within because the inner self was somehow damaged or repressed. Indeed, the German philosopher Immanuel Kant (1724–1804) linked cancer with inhibited passions, thus providing fuel for the myth that one is responsible for one's own disease.[21] And a disease caused by the repression of emotions leads to shame.

In art and in the popular imagination cancer remains the disease of the repressed. Cancer is a disease of those who have quashed their emotion and desire. Childless women have suppressed their life energy, thereby becoming useless and cancer-prone. The Austrian-American psychiatrist and psychoanalyst Wilhelm Reich (1897–1957) defined cancer as 'a disease following emotional resignation – a bio-energetic shrinking, a giving up of hope'.[22] Reich linked his thoughts about cancer and emotional resignation to the work of Freud, especially his work on sexual repression.

W. H. Auden's poem 'Miss Gee' illustrates very dramatically the link in the popular imagination between cancer and sexual repression. In the poem, Miss Gee has long harboured secret feelings of desire for the vicar of her local church. But she has never expressed her feelings for him, never allowed herself to be herself, instead sitting 'with her clothes buttoned up to her neck'. She is found to have advanced cancer and her doctor expresses his view on the disease thus:

> 'It's like some hidden assassin
> Waiting to strike at you.
>
> 'Childless women get it
> And men when they retire;
> It's as if there had to be some outlet
> For their foiled creative fire.'

Cancer is the unknown enemy, caused by failure to express yourself. The result of this repression is an invasion with cancer where one is quickly taken over and killed. Miss Gee dies quickly and the poem ends tragically:

> They took Miss Gee to the hospital,
> She lay there a total wreck,
> Lay in the ward for women
> With her bedclothes right up to her neck.
>
> They lay her on the table,
> The students began to laugh;
> And Mr. Rose the surgeon
> He cut Miss Gee in half.

But let us be clear: there are no papers published by clinical oncologists to support the idea that cancer is linked to personality.

Many happy, well-adjusted people die of the disease. The ideas that underpin these metaphors, the cancer taboo, were born in an age before we knew about viruses and genes. The idea that cancer itself is synonymous with evil, a result of personality, a judgement on behaviour is simply a 'cheap shot'.[23] But despite our more modern and scientific approach, the cancer taboo remains part of the landscape today and continues to do damage.

Although we now know that cancer is a genetic illness, caused by a combination of environment, genes and random luck, the effects of the cancer taboo can still be seen all around us. However, it's up to us how we want to define our experience and which metaphors to use – you may find the war metaphor empowering, or you may have your own images and words that you want to use. I have chosen the metaphor of journey and Christianized it into a cancer pilgrimage which defies the taboo and opens up the possibilities for a creative place of encounter with God. The next stage in our preparation is to examine ideas about self-identity and consider how this journey through the land of cancer with God might affect who we think we are.

Who do you think you are?

If the popularity of the BBC television programme *Who Do You Think You Are?* is anything to go by, we are very interested in the question of identity. In the show, celebrities discover their own family tree, exploring rumours about long-dead relatives and the journeys that they embarked upon. But the programme often reveals more than a mere genealogy: the singer finds out that he comes from a long line of musicians, or a whimsical and romantic love for the ocean is traced back to a seafaring ancestor. It can be a fascinating process to watch, not just for the stories and the history, but for the 'Eureka' moments of realization for the celebrities as they understand themselves better by looking at those who went before them.

Simply put, our identity is who we are. We know intuitively what identity is, but the definitions vary wildly and the more that we think about the idea, the more complicated the word seems to become.

The *Oxford English Dictionary* defines 'identity' in the following way:

> The sameness of a person or thing at all times or in all circumstances; the condition or fact that a person or thing is itself and not something else; individuality, personality.[24]

But does this rather bureaucratic definition really grasp how we understand our identity, which is about individual details (I am tall, from Scotland and love hill walking) but is also related to our context (I live in London, I worship in an Anglican church and have two children)? The complexity of identity issues is noticeable when you think about how you introduce yourself: it is almost always context dependent. For example, at a children's playgroup, I would introduce myself with my first name and the names of my children. In a work situation, I might use my full name and title, and give a job description. On holiday, I would introduce myself with my family and perhaps explain where I have come from. In all these situations, I wouldn't say that my core identity changes, but how I describe my identity does.

Our identity incorporates the stories we tell about ourselves, how and where we live, our bodies and what we do with them. As a concept it is often broken down into personal and social identity. Personal identity consists of those distinguishing characteristics which may include our bodies, attributes, beliefs, motivations, style, desires, principles, job and goals. It usually includes particular aspects of ourselves, but not just any and every fact. For example, I have a large and a small bowel, but I don't usually mention them in relation to questions of identity in the same way that I refer to my unusual height and my love of the Scottish mountains. But if something happens to change my body in a particular way, for example an accident or disease, then it becomes an important factor in our identity.

Our social identity is about how we identify ourselves within the community, usually through membership of some group – for example, national and ethnic identity, sexual orientation and political views. These groups also include labels such as mother, or our job description and religious faith. Identity is a fluid and complex concept, both personal and communal, solid yet open to change. Indeed, these definitions are hard to agree upon. It's as if identity itself is something ineffable, even sacred.

A cancer diagnosis has the potential to affect many areas of our identity, both in the short and the long term, in several ways. Table 1 illustrates some of the factors in identity and how cancer might affect them.

Table 1 The impact of cancer on categories of identity

Identity category	Impact of cancer
Physical identity	Disease and treatment may have substantial physical effects. For example, hair loss with chemotherapy, or loss of a breast and reconstruction. Boundaries of the body are regularly transgressed by the use of needles and scans.
Our habits, what we like to do and places we like to be	The disease and its treatment may restrict movement: there may be lots of hospital appointments, we may have to stay in bed or be isolated from others due to worries about infection. We may not be able to travel, work or interact 'normally'.
The stories that we tell about our lives	Our story now involves a cancer diagnosis, with all that means for our concerns for family and the future. People may look at us differently now that our story has changed.
Social and geographical place	We may need to spend time in hospital. Changes to work patterns or loss of employment are possible. Friendships and other relationships may change.

You are now joining a new group: those who have been diagnosed with cancer, the *cancer community*. And although a cancer diagnosis concerns a single body and a single life, its effects resonate throughout the web of communal relationships that are part of our identity. People close by, and even those far removed, can be profoundly affected by a cancer diagnosis. Relationships are always dynamic and responsive, and so cancer may affect them in profound and lasting ways.

An important aspect of identity is belief and faith. It has an impact on daily life, on action, on our passions and on our under-standing of the future. For some faith is explicit and well articu-lated; for others it is quieter, a more intangible part of their identity. Either way, it is important to explore what it means to identify ourselves as Christians, however that identity might be expressed, within the cancer journey.

It is hard to come up with a succinct definition of the Christian identity. Centrally, it is to do with the acceptance of Jesus Christ as the Word and Son of God, the Lord and Saviour of the world, fully God and fully human. But the Christian identity also includes ideas relating to how the Bible is interpreted, the history of the Church and the doctrines of God and Creation. It contains social ideas about being part of the body of Christ through baptism and communal ideas about the worship of God; it conveys practices such as personal prayer and contemplation and the ethical and practical aspects of living and loving. And just as being a Christian touches on nearly all aspects of personal identity, so will a cancer journey be no less important in working out who Christ is for us today.

There are two particular aspects of Christian theology that will be useful to pack in our bag as we prepare to set out on our can-cer journey. The first is to do with our physical bodies and the second concerns the importance of relationship in the Christian faith.

The Christian faith is not squeamish about bodies, nor does it see them as a hindrance in the spiritual life.[25] Christ himself was both fully man and fully God; he got hungry and angry, he cried and he was in pain on the cross. God's experience on earth in Jesus Christ was a bodily experience, as for instance Jesus' phys-ical reaction to the death of his friend shows us: 'Jesus began to weep' (John 11.35).

Following the resurrection, the early Church was therefore obliged to understand how it was possible that God, normally understood as eternal, changeless and free from suffering, could be the Father of Jesus Christ. Some early sects of Christianity tried to explain the uncomfortable and messy body of Christ by downplaying the physical, and saying that God was only pretending to be human. Other sects tried to pin all the problems of being human on the physical body, espousing ideas that to be spiritual it was necessary to leave the body behind and seek transcendence. Neither view was accepted by the Church and taken into mainstream thought. Jesus was truly man and truly God, as the Creeds of the Church affirm.

In the first creation narrative, when God created the whole universe including human beings he announced that it was all 'very good' (Genesis 1.31). There is no hint that earth, stars, trees, animals and human bodies are anything except 'very good'. Indeed, human beings are understood to be not mind and soul stuck together, like the batteries inside a toy, but rather an integrated whole. Much modern-day psychology will agree that our minds and the state of our physical bodies are intimately related to one another. Bodies are important because they are the way we exist in the world. We need them for communication, they are the meeting place and the medium through which our inner lives are expressed. They are where we write stories of love.

So, in terms of the journey ahead, let's pack in our bag two important ideas about the body from Christian theology. First, a key feature of Christology: God in Jesus was in a real body, a body that loved, served, suffered and died. Second, we affirm our bodies knowing that whatever happens to them, they are *very good* in the eyes of God, like the rest of creation. Our bodies are never a hindrance or a barrier to our spiritual life; we are in fact made and asked to live in the image of God (Genesis 1.27).

The second aspect of Christian faith that is central to the journey of cancer concerns relationship. We are not to think of ourselves as isolated people journeying alone; we know that we are involved in numerous webs of relationships through our friends, families and colleagues. We also know by faith that we are created by God, we relate to God in prayer, we understand ourselves as Christians within a local or global community and we are connected to others through love. All this reflects something more profound. We identify ourselves within relationship, because God is relationship. God, the Holy Trinity, Father, Son and Holy Spirit, is utterly interconnected. We know that God is love, and thus it is in love that we find God and our true identity. We journey not alone, but in that profound relationship of love as understood in the Holy Trinity.

The mystics are always best at getting to the heart of such complex ideas. Mechthild von Magdeburg (1212–77) was a medieval mystic who wrote extensively of her experiences and what they taught her about God. Here, in a dialogue between the soul and God, she writes about our interrelationship with God, and how it is through love alone that all self-knowledge and knowledge about God is gained:

> Since God no longer wanted to be in himself, he made the soul and gave himself to her out of great love. Of what are you made, soul, that you rise so high over all creatures, and mingle with the Holy Trinity and yet remain wholly in yourself? – You have spoken of my origin, now I tell it to you truly: I was made in that place from love, therefore no creature can satisfy me according to my noble nature, and no creature can unlock me, except love alone.[26]

The journey ahead is taken both within the relationships of friendship and family, and within the relationship that we have with God. And so we pack into our bag the Trinitarian love of God, just as St Patrick did in this early Celtic Christian poem:

> I arise today
> Through a mighty strength,
>   the invocation of the Trinity,
> Through belief in the Threeness,
> Through confession of the Oneness
>   of the Creator of creation.
> Christ with me,
> Christ before me,
> Christ behind me,
> Christ in me,
> Christ beneath me,
> Christ above me,

Christ on my right,
Christ on my left,
Christ when I lie down,
Christ when I sit down,
Christ when I arise,
Christ in the heart of every man who thinks of me,
Christ in the mouth of everyone who speaks of me,
Christ in every eye that sees me,
Christ in every ear that hears me.

Christ's journey to the cross is a journey of love and suffering for the salvation of the world. Many scholars have seen the four Passion narratives as early journey texts, where pilgrims in Jerusalem would have physically moved around the sites of the story acting out the events of a Passion liturgy. Sometimes today we see this acted out as the 'way of the cross' during Holy Week.

In our cancer journey, we make a parallel pilgrimage around the sites of Jesus' Passion: the Garden of Gethsemane where he struggled to accept his future, the cross where he suffered and died, the tomb where he rose again. In the following chapters, I shall take the biblical stories, Christian theology and the liturgy of Holy Week and put them into a critical conversation with the events of the cancer journey: diagnosis, treatment and what comes next. Into this dialogue I shall add my own story of cancer. This is not to be indulgent, but rather it is the foundation upon which this book is built. Furthermore, I have found healing and trans-formation in taking seriously what I could learn through my own experience and story; when I attempted to make sense of how my identity had been changed by cancer, I did so by putting it along-side the stories of the faith. For there is something important in taking very seriously the stories of our bodies, and trusting that from them theology and resurrection may emerge. And so in what follows the medical and theological is blended with the personal and biblical, in what I hope is a landscape into which your own story of cancer may be introduced and used to find healing.

As we now begin our pilgrimage, if there is one key lesson to be drawn from Jesus' own journey at the end of his life it is this:

suffering does not separate us from God. What lies ahead might be perilous, but we begin well equipped with science, theology and faith. For each of us the terrain is different, but we aim to retain the vision that we journey to seek God, knowing that God is to be found everywhere, even in the NHS waiting room or on the surgeon's table. We journey to seek the pearl in the experience, safe in the knowledge that we do not journey alone but are held by God in love.

2

Diagnosis

———•◦•———

God our Father,
your Son Jesus Christ was obedient to the end
and drank the cup prepared for him:
may we who share his table
watch with him through the night of suffering
and be faithful.
Amen.

Collect for Maundy Thursday,
Common Worship: Times and Seasons, *p. 296*

Surely, you behold trouble and misery;
you see it and take it into your own hand.

Psalm 10.14

By the rivers of Babylon –
    there we sat down and there we wept
    when we remembered Zion.

Psalm 137.1

God saw everything that he had made, and indeed, it was
very good.

Genesis 1.31

God is present at the point where the eyes of those who
give and those who receive meet.

Simone Weil

It begins

Now before the festival of the Passover, Jesus knew that his hour had come to depart from this world and go to the Father. Having loved his own who were in the world, he loved them to the end.

John 13.1–2

Jesus' journey had reached a critical point. In his ministry over the past two or three years he had been teaching about the kingdom of God, leading his group of disciples, healing and performing other miracles. He had shown them that the first shall be last by washing their feet, he had rebuked hypocrites, he had turned over the tables in the Temple and he had broken down social barriers by associating with women. He had forgiven in the name of God, and his followers believed that he was the Lord, the Son of the Most High, the Messiah for whom they had been waiting.

Then it all came crashing down: he was arrested, tortured and killed on the cross. His disciples watched in horror as their hopes fell apart and Jesus met a humiliating end. They believed that he would save them and prove himself to be the Messiah, but the cross seemed to ridicule their hopes. But then on Easter Day the resurrection ratified everything that went before: Jesus is the Saviour and his rising from the grave is the miracle upon which the Christian Church was built.

These events hinged on one night: Jesus' struggle in the Garden of Gethsemane. There, while his friends slept, he prayed that the future might be different and that he might not have to go through the cross. There he grieved and mourned the suffering he would have to face, praying for release and help. And in those lonely hours he became resolved to face the journey ahead, emerging from the Garden with his face set towards the cross, choosing in freedom to journey on in love.

The time just before a cancer journey begins can often be recalled with great clarity. It is as if everything that follows a diagnosis brings those seemingly unencumbered and worry-free days into sharper focus. It is not as if life before was perfect, it is just that the weight of a cancer diagnosis distorts everything with its enormous capacity to take attention and distract everyone from 'normal' life. So when it happens, when a cancer diagnosis crashes into a life, it divides that life into a 'before' and an 'after'. However it happens, it will almost certainly be an incredibly intense and important experience.

In the months before my diagnosis, I was working in Aberdeen, earning money for travel between climbing mountains and enjoying such summer warmth as the north-east coast of Scotland offers.

I remember the day of the walk very clearly. I had been planning a solo ascent of Lochnagar, a local Munro (a Scottish mountain over 3,000ft), for some time and had planned my route with care. It was a gloriously sunny morning that, though it started off cool, promised to heat up later. I would be guaranteed plenty of fantastic views from the top. Lochnagar is a striking amphitheatre of a mountain with a high-level loch surrounded by steep cliffs. The walk begins gently enough from the car park, down past Loch Muick, before the ascent begins through a forest. Towards the top, the walk becomes a satisfying scramble with the view improving all the time. Near the summit, on one side of the path is a beautiful, almost alpine meadow; the other is marked by a lethal cliff edge which you trace to reach the summit cairn. After reaching the top I chose to descend via a different path. This rugged scar of a trail is extremely steep and can be hazardous, but it dumps you about halfway along the north side of Loch Muick. Then there is a rather boring flat walk back to the car park which normally takes an hour or so.

I had felt strong and free as I climbed the mountain to the summit, indeed I had attracted a few puzzled stares; it is relatively unusual for a woman to climb alone in the mountains. But once I had descended and began the long slog back to the car, I began to feel incredibly tired. Indeed, I felt so drained that I was only able to trudge a few steps at a time. Exhausted and breathless, I sat down frequently, with everyone from young children to octogenarians overtaking me. I pretended to take in the view while silently doubting

whether I had any energy left to make it back to the car. Something
was deeply and seriously wrong with my body.

This was my moment, the point in time when my cancer journey
began. What was yours? Or do you know when your friend or
family member first suspected that something was wrong? It might
be a question worth asking. For me, on this very real journey
across the Scottish wilderness, a different and far tougher journey
began as I entered into worry and uncertainty, knowing that something was amiss with my body.

In this chapter, we will examine Christ's experience in the
Garden of Gethsemane as he wrestled with a future with suffering
on the horizon, and use it to explore the beginnings of a cancer
journey. Jesus' journey began in the dark, and his struggle was
real, echoing across space and time to our anguish today. It
particularly resonates with the period of cancer diagnosis, where
so much is unknown, relationships begin to change and there is
real fear.

In many churches Jesus' night of struggle in the Garden is
recalled in services on the Thursday of Holy Week, in which we
remember and recreate the evening before his arrest when he
shared a meal with his friends and broke bread. Jesus asked them
to do the same in remembrance of him, in this way instituting
the sacrament of Holy Communion. He also demonstrated to
them how they were to serve and love one another, by stooping
down and washing their feet. The service then recollects his
struggle in the Garden; this part of the service is often held in
a small chapel where the Garden is recreated with flowers and
candles. The faithful are invited to watch with Christ and to remain
with him in his struggle to accept his future.

The worship of Maundy Thursday is a catalogue of emotion,
moving from the warmth and love of a shared meal into the darkness and uncertainty of the Garden. From hope and conviviality
into solitude and fear. From normality and safety into a con-
frontation with real suffering.

I invite you to take your own experience of cancer diagnosis
into that holy night, to find resonances and glimmers of the

resurrection hope as we journey into the wilderness of cancer. We recall once more the presence of God at all times, and know that this is a well-worn path. As the transition is made from health to sickness, we journey with Christ from the upper room into the Garden. While this is happening symbolically in churches throughout the world on Maundy Thursday, it is traditional to strip the church bare. The statues are covered, the altar stripped, the candle extinguished and the lamp over the reserved sacrament blown out. There shall be no more alleluias until Easter morning. And in the darkness, words from Lamentations or verses from Psalm 88 are solemnly read out.

> O Lord, God of my salvation,
>   when, at night, I cry out in your presence,
> let my prayer come before you;
>   incline your ear to my cry . . .
> You have caused my companions to shun me;
>   you have made me a thing of horror to them.
> I am shut in so that I cannot escape;
>   my eye grows dim through sorrow.
> Every day I call on you, O Lord;
>   I spread out my hands to you.
>
>   *Psalm 88.1–2, 8–9*

Entering the wilderness

Everyone's diagnosis story is unique. Some may have had no previous symptoms, while others may have been feeling ill and worried for a long time. But in all cancer stories, there is a moment, sudden or after a long build-up, when events begin to snowball and we are ushered into a new and frightening place of uncertainty, where the scenery and landmarks are no longer recognizable.

When I listed my symptoms to Dr M. he looked concerned, and then it all began to go with worrying speed. The nurse was called back into the clinic to take a blood sample, and Dr M. asked whether I minded driving it into the hospital myself. When I arrived, I held the sample in my hand and knew that the piece of paper inside might hold a clue to the doctor's concern. It read: 'Possible Hodgkin's Lymphoma'.

I had never heard of it.

At home I looked up the disease on the internet and found that it fitted perfectly with my symptoms. I warily viewed the normal treatment: chemotherapy and radiotherapy. Although I felt panicked and scared, I also felt strangely relieved. My symptoms were not mysterious, but due to a real disease with not only a name but an associated treatment.

But it was cancer. 'Cancer'. I rolled the word around in my head. It couldn't be like other cancers, the ones that other people get? Could I have cancer? And chemotherapy – surely not me? Not the treatment that makes you go bald, pale and sick? This type of thing doesn't happen to me – this is not in my plan for my early twenties.

I waited for the results of the blood test, which were due back the following day. I soon learnt that the faster things went in hospitals, the more serious the implication.

The doctor called my work before lunch the next day. There had been a problem with my sample and he was going to refer me to the hospital.

The cancer wilderness is a strange place, where space and time behave unexpectedly. The world shrinks and suddenly all that matters is what is happening inside this one body. Time distorts, going frighteningly fast or with mind-bending slowness. You might be taken at speed through hospital tests, and then left waiting for results when days seem like months and everything is in suspended animation. It is disorientating when you first begin the journey: nothing makes sense, and 'normal' is lost. There is no security in home, or work, or routine, because cancer threatens it all. It is a strange and real wilderness: the unexpected has happened, and the abstract risk of illness becomes an acute and very personal possibility.

In the Bible, a wilderness is a barren and arid place, where nothing grows or thrives. It is a place of monsters and fear, a habitation cut off from the normal life of commerce, routine and safety. It is a frightening and chaotic place, with no easy patterns to hang on to, a place of wandering and restlessness where it is easy to get lost. The psalmist cries out to the Lord from a wilderness of disorientation and uncertainty:

> O Lord, all my longing is known to you;
>> my sighing is not hidden from you.
> My heart throbs, my strength fails me;
>> as for the light of my eyes – it also has gone from me.
> My friends and companions stand aloof from my affliction,
>> and my neighbours stand far off.
>
> *Psalm 38.9–11*

In the Hebrew Bible, the people of Israel wandered in the wilderness for forty years before entering the Promised Land and building the Temple to worship God. Before beginning his ministry and following his baptism, Jesus too entered the wilderness to wrestle with temptation (Mark 1.12; Matthew 4.1–11; Luke 4.1–13).

From neither wilderness was God ever absent. He provided manna for the Israelites, heavenly food to sustain and make them stronger in their journeying. By his nature, Jesus could never be separated from God, but the experience of temptation in the wilderness girded him with power to trust in God for strength, direction and peace.

At the end of his earthly ministry, with the Passion ahead of him, Jesus entered another wilderness in the Garden of Gethsemane to wrestle with the future that he must face. 'Gethsemane' is a corruption into English of two Hebrew words, *gat* and *shmanim*, and is taken to mean 'the place where olive oil is pressed'.

References to olive oil often signify the presence of God and olive oil is still used today to ordain priests and royalty. It was used to light up the tabernacle as the Israelites wandered in the wilderness (Exodus 27.20). When Jacob dreamt of a ladder on which angels ascended and descended between heaven and earth, signifying God's perpetual presence with his people, he awoke and poured oil over the stone upon which he had slept (Genesis 28.10–17). For the faithful, oil is holy and marks the presence of God. And, as the people of Jesus' time would have known, the harder the olives are pressed, the more oil is squeezed out.

In the immediate aftermath of a diagnosis, a transition is made into a new way of travelling, and cancer pilgrims have their passports stamped with the burdens they will carry onwards on their journey. First the role of the sufferer: you may be seriously ill, and this new part of your identity may have both real and imagined effects. Second, your ability to communicate this profound experience may prove difficult, even traumatic – more about this later. And finally, the nature of being diagnosed with a serious illness creates or shows up boundaries in space and time. Throughout much of human history, the experience of ill health and death was much more common than it is today. Now, with the advances made by modern medicine, people are living longer and death is not so much part of everyday life. But a cancer diagnosis brings us up against the coalface of our existential fragility.

The initial stages are especially difficult as we get used to this new land. For the cancer wilderness is a strange place, a threshold or liminal world, betwixt and between. It is a place of shadows, poorly lit, and it may be hard to understand the terrain in which you wander. For Christ, his liminal place was the Garden of Gethsemane, lying as it did between his active ministry among his disciples and the suffering of the cross. And when he was there he knelt and prayed, asking God for guidance about what lay ahead and trusting he would be given the strength to endure.

But we have this treasure in clay jars, so that it may be made clear that this extraordinary power belongs to God and does not come from us. We are afflicted in every way, but not crushed; perplexed, but not driven to despair; persecuted, but not forsaken; struck down, but not destroyed; always carrying in the body the death of Jesus, so that the life of Jesus may also be made visible in our bodies.

2 Corinthians 4.7–10

The present and the future

Cancer forces us into a disorientating wilderness where the pressure is real and terrifying, because it is a word and a diagnosis with a powerful message: you are not in control. Uncertainty hangs in the air: it is not as if you didn't know you are going to die, it is just that the threat of a cancer journey slaps you in the face with it.

This was the first of many trips to Aberdeen Royal Infirmary and my new life of waiting rooms. I would soon grow to abhor their plastic chairs, their depressing posters and their special power to curb normal conversation. In the waiting room my mum met someone she knew. He told her that he had been waiting months to be seen. Mum didn't mention we had only been waiting for a couple of days. I could sense the atmosphere become even more tense; we didn't say a word.

If I could summarize my thoughts at this time it might be something like, 'This can't be happening.' Or else, following John McEnroe, 'You cannot be serious!' It was like I was in a movie and it was happening to someone else, or I was having an extended out-of-body experience. I had not yet begun to relate the sickness of my body to the 'me' of my consciousness. I had not reconciled the word 'cancer', the disease I could feel on my neck and would shortly see on an X-ray, to the 'me' that enjoyed mountain climbing and was shortly to return to friends and fun in London. There was a gaping chasm between my body with cancer and who I thought I was. In tense waiting rooms, or during anxious phone calls, the struggle of bridging that aching chasm had begun.

In his garden wilderness, Christ struggled to bridge the gap between his human nature, which naturally feared suffering and death, and the divine plan which lay ahead of him. He prayed: 'Abba, Father, for you all things are possible; remove this cup from me; yet, not what I want, but what you want' (Mark 14.36).

Jesus prayed that it wouldn't happen. Despite his foreknowledge and notwithstanding his deep relationship with God the Creator of the universe, Jesus was struggling to accept the future. He didn't want to go to the cross, though he wanted to remain faithful to God. There was real tension between his life and God's plan, and Jesus feared the future.

When cancer appears on the horizon, it takes over normal life with astonishing efficiency – eating, sleeping, going out, working, everything and all time is affected by its weight. In the early moments after the Big Bang, time and space did not obey the laws of physics as we now understand them. In the same way, when cancer explodes into a life everything stops operating normally. Cancer infects our ability to plan, to relax or to just be ordinary. It parks itself on top of us, ruins our present and clouds the future.

Stanley Hauerwas (b. 1940) is an American theologian writing widely on ethics and politics in matters concerned with the connection between human life and ideas about God, the world and the importance of narrative. He contrasts the experience of being diagnosed with a serious illness with that of being caught up in a natural disaster. In an event such as a hurricane or tsunami, he writes, we don't make strong links between the injuries we may sustain and our own, individual self-worth. But with illness it is different:

> Sickness should not exist because we think of it as something in which we can intervene and which we can ultimately eliminate. Sickness challenges our most cherished presumption that we are or at least can be in control of our existence. Sickness creates the problem of 'anthropodicy' because it challenges our most precious and profound belief that humanity has in fact become god. Against the backdrop of such a belief, we conclude that sickness should not exist.[1]

Being a victim of a natural disaster feels different from sitting in a waiting room before a diagnosis of cancer. Ill health is so much more personal: we feel it should not happen, and that it is an insult when it does. It feels like a disappointment rather than a random act of nature, a personal attack and an infringement of our right to dictate what happens to us rather than a scientifically understood, though terrible, occurrence. But just like an earthquake or a flood, it undermines our foundations and the architecture of our life – not only in the present, but also as we look ahead and find that cancer has taken away our ability to plan with confidence.

There is future instability but the present moment is not without its frustrations. Indeed the extreme and the mundane are happy bedfellows in the wilderness of cancer, especially in the early stages. There are many waiting rooms and plastic chairs on the immediate horizon and this journey requires that you very quickly become good at waiting: cancer patients need patience.

Back in the Garden, Jesus waits. Waits for a new plan. Waits for help and comfort. Jesus waits on the Lord.

> I wait for the LORD, my soul waits,
>   and in his word I hope;
> my soul waits for the Lord
>   more than those who watch for the morning,
>   more than those who watch for the morning.
>
> *Psalm 130.5–6*

In the Garden

To the medical world, a human body is often thought of as a machine to be studied and repaired, and it is astounding in its complexity – there are more neural connections in one human brain than there are stars in the entire universe! Yet the body is also where and how each of us loves, and laughs, and exists as a child of God. Modern psychology and medicine recognize what the Bible has long proclaimed, that body and mind are united, an integrated 'me' known, loved and delighted in by the Creator God. The body may be the focus of cancer treatment and attention, but it is a quite extraordinary 'thing' to be going on this journey.

'Gillian Straine, please.'

I was called for my appointment quickly and went alone to see a very abrupt consultant: 'Yup, yup, yup,' he said, flicking through some notes. Lifting my top to allow him to poke my spleen and then my lymph glands, he announced: 'Probably Hodgkin's. Best get you to X-ray, you know, just to be sure.'

I retrieved my mum, and we followed the signs to find our way to the imaging department, a thin, new patient folder in my hand.

I changed into a gown, and was asked to stand pressing myself against a cold metal surface for the X-ray to be taken. I was handed the image, and asked to carry it myself back to the original clinic. I held it up to the light and squinted at my chest cavity, just like I had seen on the TV, but could see nothing amiss. But, on my return to the first clinic, the rude consultant said, 'Yup, yup, yup, Hodgkin's,' poking the apple-sized lump I had missed in my chest cavity. 'Best get you up to Haematology,' he announced.

I needed to have a biopsy of the large lump in my neck. The extraction of lymph nodes is generally done under a general anaesthetic but I screwed up my nose at that idea, and gladly agreed to the doctor's tentative suggestion of performing it under a local anaesthetic.

Again, I was alarmed at the speed at which events were unfolding around me at the hospital. I was immediately found a bed in a day surgery unit and taken promptly to theatre. I was given some sedatives and told that if I felt anything they would simply put in more local anaesthetic. I remember lying in the operating theatre talking to the handsome anaesthesiologist, with the slight, though not unpleasant feeling that I was repeating myself.

Whisked through recovery, and then home. Thoroughly investigated and poked, I awaited what I felt was inevitable.

In the diagnosis process, a transition is made: from the 'normal' world into the medical world. In this world, the person with cancer becomes a cancer patient, a body of enormous interest to trained professionals.

This transition may be compared to the one Jesus went through in the Garden, from someone leading a ministry and inspiring his followers, to someone under arrest, whose physical body became the property of the state. 'After Jesus had spoken these words, he went out with his disciples across the Kidron valley to a place where there was a garden, which he and his disciples entered' (John 18.1).

After words of love and the command to serve, Jesus went to wait for the future. He chose to wait in a garden, in a place of nature. In the Bible, when nature flourishes God is present and there may be symbolic reasons why Jesus chose this place. But it is also normal to want to be in the natural environment; we feel grounded and whole in green places, for God may be glimpsed in the fragility and balance of the natural world. From this place of beauty, Jesus was arrested, bound and taken away towards an interrogation; he no longer had any control: 'Then they seized him and led him away, bringing him into the high priest's house' (Luke 22.54).

Hospitals are anonymous places where we are stripped of our individuality. 'You' are a referral letter from a GP. 'You' are a list of symptoms. 'You' are a folder with your name and hospital number at the front. 'You' are opened up and examined via tests and scans. 'You' are a potential diagnosis.

'Probably Hodgkin's' was why I was there, but it didn't sum me up. It failed to mention my interest in outdoor sports, my obsession with French macarons and my rather unusual hair colour. These didn't matter. I was there for one reason only. But inevitably, and for very good reasons, in the beginnings of a diagnosis and the entry into the wilderness of cancer and ill health, there is a stripping down and a reduction in personhood.

Your body has boundaries and in the diagnosis process they are trampled over. Needles are poked into your arms to extract blood; scans look inside you, producing encoded information about your body. This is a non-hostile takeover of what was once your own, beautiful precious body, which you do lovely things with like long walks, delicious meals and that first kiss. Now it is sucked into a medical system and asked to dress in humiliating, anonymous gowns with ribbons in the wrong places, and there is a folder all about your body containing writing that you don't understand. The cold and dark of Christ's Garden experience has strong echoes in the doctors' surgeries where this information is decoded and we learn the future of our own precious selves.

Hospitals whip us away from all that is natural and we have to take our beautiful, ill bodies to new places as we are thrust into the medical system. There is much new information to take on board, new routines and a multitude of appointments. Pot plants and well-thumbed magazines will never make a hospital waiting room anything like home. Arms placed on pillows for blood tests, the gathering of bags of drugs from the pharmacy, the learning of a new language of cannulas and infusion machines: this is a new land, with a new language, strange customs and experiences.

But the wise cancer pilgrim remembers one secret: we are a body and soul all mixed into one (even if it is not mentioned in the medical notes). The experiences of your body as it goes from department to department, the file ever thickening, is yours and yours alone. A cancer diagnosis which leads you into a medicalized wilderness can produce an earthquake, a seismic shift in identity, but never one from which God is absent. Just because something has happened and our bodies are ill, doesn't mean that we need to leave them behind or feel negative towards them.

Simone Weil (1909–43), the French mystical philosopher, makes this point about the neutrality and beauty of nature: 'The sea is not less beautiful in our eyes because we know that sometimes ships are wrecked by it.'[2] It is an observation that we can transfer to the finely balanced natural machine that is our body: the body is not less beautiful because sometimes it gets cancer; the complexity and splendour of biology is not diminished by the fact that it may go wrong; the beauty and integrity of a human body is no less important and amazing because it gets sick; the ill body is not loved less than the healthy body in the eyes of the one who created it.

For it was you who formed my inward parts;
you knit me together in my mother's womb.
   I praise you, for I am fearfully and wonderfully made.
Wonderful are your works;
   that I know very well.
My frame was not hidden from you, when I was being made
   in secret,
   intricately woven in the depths of the earth.
Your eyes beheld my unformed substance.
In your book were written all the days that were formed for me,
   when none of them as yet existed.

Psalm 139.13–16

Emotions

Cancer may be a disease with its origins in cell biology, but its power to transcend its boundaries is almost without limit. How we respond to a diagnosis of cancer emotionally, and how we use and experience these emotions in the journey ahead, is a key part of the cancer pilgrimage.

> Once, only once did I cry; loud racking sobs into my handbag while Mum got a ticket for the car park. But mostly it was silence, stunned silence, behind thin cubicle curtains in hospital departments as I travelled around gathering a diagnosis.
>
> My emotions made themselves felt later during my treatment, when I lost it completely in a café – they didn't have the cake I wanted and the injustice of it all came crashing down. I refused to eat, shaking, unable to speak except for deafening expletives. I feel terrible now for projecting so much on to the open-mouthed waitress who perhaps guessed there was something else going on underneath my bald head and scarf.
>
> And another time after treatment was finished, when I was in a bookshop and I read a poem almost accidentally. Suddenly great sobs swelled in my chest, and they could no longer remain hidden. I found a corner and stayed there, bawling, collapsing under the weight of unexpressed emotions while others continued to browse.
>
> But for me, this all came later. For now, I sat staring agape at a future I couldn't imagine, and there was only silence and disbelief.

It is a stereotype, but there are truths in stereotypes: the British don't do emotion. We like to keep a stiff upper lip and not let the world know how we are really feeling. Indeed, showing too much emotion, especially of a negative kind, may be perceived as a sign of weakness. Tears and anger make people uncomfortable and there is a sense that they are best kept away from public gaze, and preferably allowed out, if at all, in the privacy of your own home. We can repress with the best.

But keeping emotions under wraps was certainly not one of Jesus' characteristics. He cried when his friend died; he got angry when people were abusing the Temple; and during his ministry he was moved on more than one occasion by compassion. Jesus was unafraid to feel and to let those feelings promote action.

His time in the Garden of Gethsemane was full of emotion. Indeed, the whole scene was fraught, with the anguished figure of the Christ pleading with the Father to take away the cup of suffering that he was being given, and returning to his friends for support only to find them asleep. Three times he prayed in torment to God to change the future path that he knew lay ahead, and three times when he turned to his friends for comfort they were unavailable.

Jesus' fear about his future was an embarrassment to some in the early Church. Later Gospels try to water it down, and reduce his fears – indeed Augustine couldn't accept the cry of Jesus from the cross, linking it with Adam, the first man, crying to God and not to the redeemer of Adam's sin. But it is there in the first four Gospels: he was in agony as he struggled to accept what was to happen: 'And he said to them, "I am deeply grieved, even to death . . ."' (Mark 14.34).

Theologians wrangle over the nature of this suffering. God is traditionally understood to be unchanging or 'impassible', therefore if Jesus was the son of God, 'of one being with the Father', how could he not have known his own future? There are different explanations. Perhaps it was just the human bit of Jesus that feared. Or perhaps the anguish was caused by the difficulty of loving like God in this fallen place. Hans von Balthasar wrote that Jesus' suffering in the Garden echoes the degree of his love for God and humankind: 'The stronger the love is, the more painful are the wounds of co-suffering.'[3]

Whatever the reason, Jesus struggled here and was unrestrained in expressing his emotions. If there is one theological lesson to be learnt, this is it – God is OK with our emotions, even the overwhelmingly negative ones. If Jesus, the God-man, cried in despair in the Garden, then it is perfectly fine for those who believe and trust in God to do so at difficult moments of life.

For there is real anger to be faced in a cancer diagnosis. It may be subverted into other emotions like sadness or grief, or converted into displacement actions like shopping, or cleaning, or eating, but there is a place for righteous anger and it is OK for it to be expressed. Cancer changes your present and your future: you are not in control entirely, and you might die from the disease. This is not in 'The Plan' for your life, and it is OK to be furious about it.

In the suffering that lies ahead, there is a danger of cutting yourself off and getting lost within an inexpressible vale of emotions, to your own detriment. For the anger will be there whether we like it or not: dealing with it is both healthy and a theological mandate. A good first attempt at addressing your anger is by doing what people have always done: have a moan and let it out. If the exiled people of Israel sat by the rivers of Babylon and wept, then so can we. They mourned what they had lost and felt abandoned, far from hope and promise. The Psalms are full of complaint and anger rising out of periods of suffering, pain and profound disorientation, and they are a great source for accessing our own emotions. For example, in the following quotation the psalmist shouts at God and demands that God should keep his promise to care for his faithful people:

> Rouse yourself! Why do you sleep, O Lord?
> Awake, do not cast us off for ever!
> Why do you hide your face?
> Why do you forget our affliction and oppression?
> *Psalm 44.23–24*

Lament is an ancient way of singing the pain and communicating the depths of the horrors of suffering. Modern versions abound, and anywhere that a conversation is being held or a tear shed with friends, anywhere people are telling their stories without being afraid of the emotions released, is a place of healing. Dorothee Soelle was a German theologian who linked experience of God with action and liberation. She writes of the importance of suffering being a vehicle of connection not only with God, but with the energy to act and use the suffering to promote real change:

'If people cannot speak about their affliction they will be destroyed by it, or swallowed up by apathy.'[4]

For Soelle, when suffering is expressed, whether in tears or lament or anger, then healing begins and we find ourselves at the start of a process where identity is reformed positively out of places of horror and pain.

So now, in the wilderness of diagnosis, where all is new and unexpected, bask in lament: use it and live it. For therein lies the way out of this place. In all but one of the psalms of lament, there is movement from the negative into the praise of God. Every time a psalm is begun in real human rage, it always ends in the same place, because one single hope remains eternal, whether or not you feel it: God is with us and there is hope.

> Rise up, come to our help.
> Redeem us for the sake of your steadfast love.
> *Psalm 44.26*

But at a distance

We know who we are through how we relate to others, to the world and to God. Theologically, God is relation expressed in the Holy Trinity, and we are made in God's image. We are all about relationship from beginning to end. The way that a diagnosis affects the webs of relationships that surround us is one of the key aspects of the cancer pilgrimage. And it is also one of the hardest parts of the journey: we travel alone as cancer pilgrims, while we are surrounded by others who travel with us, through pain and suffering, only at a distance.

No one gives you a handbook about how to handle things like telling a parent that you have a life-threatening illness, but I think I did pretty badly. While I was waiting, in another waiting room, I said very quietly, 'They think it might be cancer, you know.' And then I promptly disappeared to get X-rayed.

Over the next few days I contacted my bosses, popped into work to clear my desk and sent group emails to let people know what was happening. I don't know what I was expecting, but all the replies and responses felt disappointing. I didn't want to be doing this, and no one wanted to receive such news or have to think of a reply.

I felt as if I was on an island that was rising higher above the water, and I was growing more distant from all those who knew and loved me. I was protecting them and they were protecting me. More was left unsaid than said. We shored up our resources, girded ourselves and shut the doors. Relationships were put on hold; no one was quite sure how to proceed.

As the early days of diagnosis transitioned into confirmation, I was moving between worlds: from the domain of the well to the realm of the ill. And as more people found out, as the cards and flowers arrived, they had almost the opposite effect to the love in which they were sent. I would be going through the process with all the devotion and support of my wonderful family, but ultimately this was my body, my future, and I had to do it alone.

Cancer is a disease caused by the uncontrolled division of cells which may eventually spread around the whole body. In a similar way, a diagnosis of cancer is never an isolated event, but its effects ripple out into the community of people who surround the person who is ill. Your cancer diagnosis, the state of your physical body and the changes to your future inflicted by that diagnosis, shakes the foundations of many people's lives. Those closest to you are most deeply affected, but do not underestimate how far-reaching the effects might be. Looking ahead into the future, you may continue to be affected by other people's diagnoses, people you know or others in the media or public life. Your own life affects others, and you are in the 'Cancer Club' now. Cancer is personal and no diagnosis will leave you unmoved.

People react in different ways. Some run away and do not want to talk about it. Others get very upset and look to you for comfort. A few say just the right thing. There will be a number who ask for statistics on survival, or tell you some variation of: 'You'll fight it. You are strong.' Others may recommend diets or tell you stories about people they know who have survived – or died from – the cancer you have. Managing this maelstrom is a significant early experience of a cancer diagnosis, and it may be wise to look to your close friends and family to help you manage with responding to these communications, and keeping on top of updates and the dissemination of news.

But although a cancer diagnosis is almost a community event, it is widely reported to be a lonely disease, as described by Audre Lorde in her account of being treated for breast cancer.

> The status of untouchable is a very unreal and lonely one, although it does keep everyone at arm's length, and protects as it insulates. But you can die of that specialness, of the cold, the isolation. It does not serve living. I began quickly to yearn for the warmth of the fray, to be good as the old even while the slightest touch meanwhile threatened to be unbearable.[5]

At this point in your journey into the cancer wilderness, the fact is that you do not know whether you will survive. The statistics may be favourable; the medical care astoundingly advanced; the doctors may be positive, your family gunning for you. But nothing and no one can offer guarantees: there is no ultimate earthly comfort, as Lisa Lynch writes in her book *The C-Word*: 'But even being surrounded by my favourite people in the world felt hopelessly lonely, because nobody knew what it was like to be stuck in my tortured mind and my useless body – nor was I keen to tell them.'[6]

When Christ entered the Garden he was with his friends, and he asked them to wait and watch with him as he left them to pray (Luke 22.41). While he struggled, wrestling in anguish with the future he had to face on behalf of the human race, his friends let him down by falling asleep not once, but three times. He did it alone. 'Then he came to the disciples and found them sleeping; and he said to Peter, "So, could you not stay awake with me one hour?"' (Matthew 26.40).

Like the distance between Christ and his companions, we feel at a distance from our own lives, our hopes, our plans and our friends, and this can cause loneliness and isolation. This isn't the good solitude of spiritual journeying, but the enforced horror of subjugation to a lonely and unwanted situation.

But there may be moments and glimmers of human comfort and hope, and through such as these God's presence will shine. Just like the comfort that Jesus received from angels in Luke's version of the Garden scene (Luke 22.43–44), so too we will be sent comfort and friendship in the darkness and uncertainty of these early days.

> Over the weekend as I awaited the final test results I went with my parents to the Edinburgh Festival, sleeping on the camp bed in their hotel room. It seems a bizarre thing to have done, given the news we were waiting for, but there was a certain power and security in carrying on as normal. I was having quite severe symptoms of Hodgkin's by this time, and don't really remember much of the New York State Ballet performance, which I sweated and itched my way through, with a large bandage on my neck hidden beneath a scarf. For some reason, I remember a barista in Starbucks who asked how I was and with whom I had a chat. Someone promised to visit from London. I went out with a friend for a meal and to the cinema. She responded to what I needed, talking about it when I brought it up, while the rest was gossip and food.

There may be moments of normality that keep us afloat, a kind word that transforms the horror into an ordinary, human event or a time of forgetting and laughter. We need to remain open to these flashes, for in them we entertain the love that is always present to us.

Rise, let us be going

Whatever the precise outcome of the period of diagnosis, it usually has a clear ending: cancer is confirmed and there is no turning back from the journey that lies ahead.

> Mum and Dad were at work when the phone rang. The doctor said I had to come in to get the results but I pressed him to tell me over the phone.
> 'I am sorry, but . . .'
> I had cancer.

Just as dawn has to follow the night's darkness, so too Jesus could not remain for ever in the Garden. So what had happened there? What had changed for Jesus in the prayer and solitude, in the anguish and despair? What difference did that night make to the journey that lay ahead of him?

In the poem 'The Garden of Olives', Rainer Maria Rilke dispenses with any idea that Jesus was given special divine comfort in Gethsemane, or indeed any relief from nature or the darkness of night:

> Later it was said: an angel came –.
>
> Why an angel? Alas it was the night
> leafing indifferently among the trees.
> The disciples stirred in their dreams.
> Why an angel? Alas it was the night.
>
> The night that came was no uncommon night;
> hundreds like it go by.
> Then dogs sleep, and then stones lie.
> Alas a sad night, alas any night
> that waits till it be morning once again.[7]

For Rilke, the night of Jesus' struggle relates to every experience of suffering when someone is conscious of dying, or when people are facing pain or feeling that their certainty in God is destroyed. Jesus went through it in the Garden, and emerged the next morning. But he did more than just pray until morning; something changed. In his 'Rise, let us be going', addressed to his sleepy disciples, he affirmed that his face was now set towards the cross and to all the suffering that lay ahead. Similarly, Dorothee Soelle, reflecting on the events of that night, writes: 'The cup of suffering becomes the cup of strengthening. Whoever empties that cup has conquered all fear.'[8]

The Garden was not just a place of darkness, but a place of transition which ended in determination. Jesus may have begged that the cup of suffering be taken away, but he left the Garden having drunk from it, and found in the dregs the resolve to walk into the future that awaited him. The Garden had been worth it, and in Jesus' departure from the Garden to face the cross, this scene displays that a Christian life is not diminished by the reality of suffering.

Whatever the reasons for pain – and here is not the place for a theological discussion of why God allows suffering – it is part of the reality when we face a cancer diagnosis. How that pain is handled is important if we are to find the meaning in the experience. Frequently in the Psalms, the words of lament, anger and demand are turned to praise, and they pivot on one theological point: God exists. Just like Christ, we are never left in the hopelessness of the Garden, never abandoned to fear; not for a second are we lost. As St Paul writes:

> For I am convinced that neither death, nor life, nor angels, nor rulers, nor things present, nor things to come, nor powers, nor height, nor depth, nor anything else in all creation, will be able to separate us from the love of God in Christ Jesus our Lord.
>
> *Romans 8.38–39*

But there is more in the emergence of Christ from the Garden that is pertinent to moving from cancer diagnosis to face the treatment that lies ahead. When Christ went forward, strengthened by his dark night in the Garden, it is interesting to note what he did not do. He didn't launch into clever speeches. He didn't overturn tables. He didn't lead great gatherings. In fact, he didn't do much at all, except hand himself over to be arrested. At that moment, his body was taken by the state and he became passive to what lay ahead. He let others do unto him, and through his passivity and letting be he let the glory of God shine through in the events that followed.

It is not possible to fight, build or bargain a way out of the cancer wilderness. When we are there we don't *do* much, rather we let the medical system treat our bodies. Of course, this is not to deny that it is important to eat well, avoid infection, and seek comfort in our friendships and relationships. But, on a deeper level, it is perhaps important to recognize that we do not have complete control. The very nature of both the disease and the various treatments that we may be offered demands a degree of passivity; a passivity in which Christ participates ahead of us, and for our salvation.

In Gethsemane, the place where oil is pressed, a man was given the power to drink the cup of suffering and set his face in freedom to what lay ahead. It was the place of struggle and horror as an unimaginable future rose, but one that was accepted as the light of dawn on Good Friday broke. In the cancer wilderness a diagnosis is made. The doctor looks down, and says, 'I am sorry but . . .' The wait is over, the worry and fear can be focused now and translated into action. The diagnosis is our passport into the world of the ill, and the medical system begins to direct us towards the paths that need to be taken in the wilderness ahead. The future remains unclear, but for now there is consolation and the diagnosed find strength in knowledge, in the system and in the awareness that they never travel alone. The cup is accepted and drained, and the strength of Christ is ours.

> Do not forsake me, O LORD;
> O my God, do not be far from me;
> make haste to help me,
> O Lord, my salvation.
>
> *Psalm 38.21–22*

3

Treatment

———◆——◆——◆———

Let us pray for all those who suffer:
   for those who are deprived and oppressed,
   for all who are sick,
   for those in darkness, in doubt and in despair, in loneliness
      and in fear,
   for prisoners, captives and refugees,
   for the victims of false accusations and violence,
   for all at the point of death and those who watch beside them,
that God in his mercy will sustain them
with the knowledge of his love.

From the Intercessions for Good Friday,
Common Worship: Times and Seasons, *p. 318*

If I say, 'Surely the darkness shall cover me, and the light
   around me become night',
even the darkness is not dark to you;
the night is as bright as the day,
for darkness is as light to you.

Psalm 139.11–12

Blessed be the God and Father of our Lord Jesus Christ,
the Father of mercies and the God of all consolation, who
consoles us in all our affliction, so that we may be able to
console those who are in any affliction with the consolation
with which we ourselves are consoled by God. For just as
the sufferings of Christ are abundant for us, so also our
consolation is abundant through Christ.

2 Corinthians 1.3–5

Leaving the Garden

> Then Jesus, knowing all that was to happen to him, came
> forward and asked them, 'For whom are you looking?'
>
> *John 18.4*

When Christ left the Garden of Gethsemane he was no longer in
control of his future; he had been betrayed and was now under
arrest and subject to the forces which surrounded him. The path
that lay ahead ran through a multiplicity of suffering: physical,
social and psychological. He would be beaten and nailed to the
cross; he would be abandoned by his friends and humiliated; he
would be lifted high on the cross; he would be condemned by the
world he came to save. He would cry out in fear, terrified that
he had been abandoned by God. This is the future he committed
himself to for us as he stepped out of the shade of the Garden
and into the glare and clamour.

In this chapter, we enter into the drama with Jesus, walking
with him through the wilderness of suffering and attempting to
remember that he travels with us as we make our own way through
treatment. For the individual handed a diagnosis of cancer, there
can be little doubt that suffering lies ahead. But uncertainty too,
vast and frightening uncertainty: how much, how deep, how long?
What will the treatment feel like? How will I cope? Who will be
standing by with me? How will cancer change me?

'I have cancer.'

It was a phrase that echoed around my head, resonating,
blocking out all other noises and distractions. At that moment,
I was alone with the knowledge and no one except me and the
doctor knew. It felt final and heavy, still unreal, too big to hold by
myself, but I knew that when I began to share it around and tell
my parents and sister, friends and colleagues, its weight would
grow and spread. Suspended, disorientated, disembodied, I held
the news. Suddenly it was real, and the little bit of me that didn't
believe that I could possibly ever have something as big and
serious as cancer was about to melt away. I was now a cancer
patient. I had cancer. And I had to tell others; it needed to spill out

and flow towards those at the sidelines. The doctor reeled off what would happen next – an appointment with a registrar, 'staging', wig fittings, dietician, Macmillan nurse, treatment . . . A seemingly well-trodden path was explained to me and it was my time now to come forward and tread it.

The crucifixion and resurrection of Jesus Christ for the salvation of the whole world was a one-off event, an unrepeatable moment in the history of the universe. Annually, on Good Friday, the Church chooses to draw itself back through the horror of Christ's arrest, crucifixion and death. Traditionally, churches are stripped of all colour, adornments and beauty. The service is subdued and quiet; there is no music or joy. Liturgically, we mirror the horror of the day – Jesus was abandoned and there are no alleluias. How quickly the adulation of Palm Sunday is forgotten. There is only loss and shock, as Christ is stripped, and lifted high on the cross as the world kills God.

We presumably don't have to put ourselves through this every year before we enjoy the Easter feast. We could stay rejoicing in safe, green fields, bathing in post-resurrection light. However, since its earliest days the Church has chosen to walk back through these terrible events again and again, asking what they mean for us and for our situation, believing that there is wisdom and peace to be found in the travelling.

While this process can never give us an exact map for travel in the land of cancer, it at least gives us a clear signpost and assurance. For Christians believe that Christ is with us today in whatever happens to us because of what he went through on Good Friday and during the resurrection. Reciprocally, when we suffer, Christian theology reflects the idea that Christ was God and a 'man of suffering acquainted with infirmity' (Isaiah 53.3a). All of the isolation, fear and real pain was part of God's experience through his Son. So whatever pain we need to deal with, when we are met with our own 'lesser Calvary' then we are assured of Christ's presence and can be certain that our suffering is held within the heart of God.

In the hour of fear: I will put my trust in you. *Psalm 56.3*

The interrogation

But Jesus was silent.   *Matthew 26.63*

From the garden, Jesus was taken back and forth between the Jews and the Romans, bouncing between political and theological agendas and accusations, as a charge was sought that would allow him to be killed. He was subject to a system, processed and taken where he did not want to go: according to the biblical accounts, Judas 'handed him over', the Jews 'delivered' him to Pilate, who 'sent him away' to Herod, who 'sent him back' and eventually he was 'delivered up to their will'. All parties interrogated him: 'Did you prophesy?' 'Did he blaspheme?' 'Are you the King of the Jews?' From the Garden, to Jew, to pagan, to death, the journey of Christ involves everyone, as we are all swept up into the drama. The Gospels paint a fraught and fractious picture, with Jesus being impelled along, bound and subject.

The speed, the passivity, the confusion and interrogation were all key aspects of Jesus' experience between the Garden and the cross, themes that I recognized in my own cancer diagnosis.

They had the blood tests, X-rays and biopsy, so the cancer was confirmed. Now they had to work out how far through my body it had spread hitherto unnoticed. For Hodgkin's lymphoma, this part of the process involved a bone marrow biopsy in the hip.

I lay on a narrow bed, covered with a paper sheet, and watched the surgeon prepare metal instruments using his body as best he could to hide my view of them. The nurse quietly asked my mum to wait outside, before turning to me and gently holding down the top half of my body. A few minutes later I knew that descriptions of the procedure that I had read on the internet had not exaggerated the bone-crunching agony. I lay on my side in shock, sweating, with iodine dripping down my legs after the doctor had finished and began to bag up his sample. He had to tell me to get dressed.

Next, another waiting room, clutching my still quite empty appointment card which was soon to be filled up like a train timetable. We sat nervously on the plastic chairs, aggressively flicking through the out-of-date magazines, waiting for the next new face, the registrar haematologist. It was a bit of a whirl, and I was later glad that I had someone with me to remember much of the detail. I might lose my hair. I might experience sickness, mouth ulcers, constipation. My fertility might be damaged.

There were options and plans, but it all seemed so uncertain and contingent in that moment: 'I might . . . It could . . . Time will tell . . .' The big question hung unasked and unanswered: what were my survival chances? Within this vast silence, questions which a month ago would have been of an order of magnitude greater than I could possibly imagine were being dealt with: how to handle hair loss, drugs to counter sickness, decisions over future family options, all made by sympathetic professionals in that airless room. In the face of a much bigger question, these seemed trivial and everyday decisions which were easily made.

For an individual approaching cancer treatment, the bit in between diagnosis and the start of treatment can be confusing and difficult – there are new people to meet, the language of cancer to learn and important decisions to be made. You will receive advice about diet and lifestyle from many sources. And there is uncertainty both as to how the treatment will affect you in the short term, and how it will work out in the long term.

As you tread the corridors of the hospital, gathering in advice and data as best you can, the news of your diagnosis is spreading abroad: first among your family and then beyond to friends, colleagues and acquaintances. Via social media, your diagnosis may be pinged all over the world in an instant. Offers of assistance flow in and people will want to help, for you are ill and despite your best hopes, your cancer will be the dominant feature of your life for quite some time.

Your news is public, similarly to the way your physical body is now the subject of scrutiny, tests and medical opinion. You may wonder at times what is going on but the information you gather and the medical professionals you see should help you come to terms with the diagnosis. But it is important to be aware that in medical systems, and for very good reasons, the temptation is to focus on the body to such an extent that the person who inhabits it gets lost, his or her identity muted.

But this is *your* body. The illness may be serious and you are probably facing months of treatment, but *you* need to embody the situation and own what is happening to you. Sometimes people name their cancer, or talk to it, however strange that might sound. For we know by faith that we are wonderfully wrought together, made in the image of God in our mother's womb (Psalm 139.13). Therefore, if God has such an interest in our physical bodies, it is important that we don't simply abandon them to the system that is going to make us well again. The doctors are highly trained and we need their help and science in healing. But in many ways we can and must retain power – so make sure that you ask questions and take the time to care for yourself. This is *your* body, a body that is loved and blessed by God, a body on a journey with Christ through difficult terrain.

In Jesus' interrogation he answered the claims of his accusers – 'You say that I am' – but admitted nothing. His power came from a higher source. Despite the ultimate claim that the state made on Jesus' body, and the suffering he faced, he never handed over ultimate control of this life. Rather, he accepted the situation, and in that acceptance found freedom.

The South American Roman Catholic Bishop Dom Helder Camara (1909–99) was a mystic involved in the political struggles of the poor and abandoned. He spent much time among those who suffered the most, and had no power. What emerges from this very different type of suffering is a universal theme: power doesn't come from earthly authorities and those who appear to have control over us. For the Christian, the real power lies elsewhere and can never be taken away, no matter how weak the powerless appear.

When I stand before customs-officers and police-commissioners,
I smile mischievously, for no one detects
the divine contraband, the stowaway,
whose highly discreet presence is visible
only to angels' glances.[1]

Scourging and mocking

They struck his head with a reed, spat upon him, and knelt
down in homage to him.   *Mark 15.19*

There is no doubt about the physicality of Jesus' suffering. He was
spat at, struck, slapped, tied up and whipped. It grieves us to read
it. He suffered in the scourging, not only physically but also emotionally and psychologically as they dressed him as a king and
pretended to worship him. He had no control over his body as
he was bound and taken where he did not wish to go; he was
degraded and in pain.

The suffering entailed in cancer treatment is multifaceted, deep
and individual.

A day later I met my oncologist, Mr C. He told me I had advanced
Hodgkin's disease. Luckily, it had not spread to the bone marrow
and so everyone was 'optimistic'. I was to begin chemotherapy
immediately and he went through all the possible symptoms
and outcomes of the treatment. Knowledge was predicated over
feelings.

I was to receive six months of chemotherapy, one session every
fortnight. At each treatment I would receive intravenously a series
of four cytotoxic drugs, the final one being administered over
several hours via a drip. Each had the potential to cause different
side effects. Aside from the hair loss, mouth pain, constipation and
tiredness that are associated with many cytotoxic treatments, these
four also carry with them a risk of heart problems, chest pain,
breathing problems and nerve damage.

I was deeply terrified. I felt sick before I even arrived and
proffered up my innocent veins for the first assault. My nurse, Jeff,
tried to put me at my ease, chatting about this and that while ever
so gently pushing the chemicals into my bloodstream. He sat in
front of me, swathed in a red plastic apron and gloves to protect
him from the drugs that everyone hoped would cure me.

He remained with me, patiently waiting, attending and watching
to make sure that I didn't have any sudden adverse reaction to
the drugs. My veins burned and I sickened. The final drug went

in over the course of about four hours. It was bright red and reacted to sunlight, and so it was draped with a black bin liner as if I was going to a Halloween party.

After about seven hours in the department, and once every last drop of the cancer-curing chemicals had entered my indignant veins, I was free to leave. The first session was over, and that night I slept well for the first time in months. Over the next few days I popped pills to counteract the side effects of the treatment.

From then on I entered into a bizarre two-weekly cycle. I would receive the chemotherapy on Friday and would feel sick and listless for a week before feeling more myself the following week. Then I would try to get out of the house and enjoy a coffee or a meal, and would try to do things that cheered me up. And then on Thursday I would have to go back to the hospital for a blood test, and on Friday I would be back in the chemotherapy suite to begin the process all over again.

I spent many hours in that grim space where good people worked hard: hours waiting for the blood test results, hoping they were OK and that I would be able to have the next dose of chemotherapy without falling behind or needing to go into hospital; hours in that dreadful waiting room, avoiding eye contact with everyone else and feeling uncomfortable as some kind person attempted to make tea for the entire group; hours trying not to look like a patient but rather like a concerned relative up until the moment when my name was called; hours waiting for the chemicals to be prepared and rushed up from the pharmacy; hours sitting in plastic padded chairs receiving those corrosive and burning drugs into my veins; hours watching the drip machine tick by, the chemicals seeping into my body as I grew increasingly pale. Those hours are seared into my mind. Tedious hours, each minute dragging by as I slowly began to feel more sick. Hours spent in various activities as I tried to no avail to distract myself. Mostly I just shut my eyes while inside I was screaming, hating that godforsaken place of suffering that I had to sit in.

Medicine and science are improving at an incredible rate, with treatments being refined and suffering reduced. More people are surviving cancer and the treatment of cancer than ever before, and important new treatments such as gene therapy are being rolled out. This is all to be celebrated.

However, for many the trusty trinity of cancer therapy remains surgery, chemotherapy and radiation. Each of these causes real physical pain and there is simply nothing to be gained in pretending otherwise. Each in its quest to cure trespasses over the normal boundaries of the human body, invited in but not without cost.

What's more, each introduces into the life of the patient a certain level of ambiguity: they will almost certainly make you feel worse in the short term in order for the cancer to be removed. The chemotherapy drugs enter the room covered with skulls and other warning symbols. The radiation sears through healthy tissue. A part of your body gets removed by the surgeon's knife. You might lose your hair temporarily or your fertility permanently. Your skin might burn, and your memory may seem to fail you. You are changed – in the short and the long term – in the endeavour to get rid of cancer.

It is perhaps in treatment that the war metaphor for cancer might resonate most powerfully. The surgeon's scalpel is a weapon of war, the machete and bayonet of hand-to-hand combat. Chemotherapy is the chemical weapon affecting the whole to cure a small outbreak of dissent. Radiation will force the unfettered multiplication into retreat. These are the sharp-edged, chemical and nuclear weapons of mass destruction deployed on the cancer patient.

It may or may not be helpful to think of treatment in this way. The ecological approach we explored earlier sees the surgery, chemicals or radiation as part of God's gift. The treatments in this model are life-saving tools developed by human minds to overcome the cancer within, the disease which is less enemy and more part of the natural order. It's the metaphor I lean towards, and everywhere I live I plant the periwinkle plant which produces a delicate splash of blue in the garden and from which was developed one of the most powerful chemotherapy drugs that I received.

However the treatment is conceived, suffering is part of it, and it is good to rail against it rather than pretend that it is not happening. Suffering is unnatural, for we are made for life and in the treatment of cancer we peek over the edge of the existential boundary of our lives and discover our own vulnerability. God will meet you here; do not be afraid to be afraid.

> Lord,
> I am tearing the soul of my heart in two.
> I need you to come
> and lie there yourself
> in the wounds of my soul
> *Mechthild von Magdeburg*

For this is a path Christ trod, in whose footsteps we now walk. St Paul wrote that we are part of the body of Christ through faith. And Christ's body is a wounded and battered one, which experienced pain and was raised with the wounds still present. We are both part of Christ's wounded body and part of this cancer world right now. As Christ was obedient to his journey, we also need to be obedient to where we are and seek God in it. Even here, in all the pain and awfulness, there is an opportunity to seek God. Pray for the grace to seek glimpses of the divine while lying on a radiation couch, or watching the needles plunge into your veins, and be awed by God who is there in front of you, holding your hand and listening to your story.

> Be thou my vision, O Lord of my heart;
> All else be naught to me save that thou art
> Thou my best thought by day or by night,
> waking or sleeping, thy presence my light.[2]

Carrying the cross

As they went out, they came upon a man from Cyrene named Simon; they compelled this man to carry his cross.

Matthew 27.32

Meanwhile, standing near the cross of Jesus were his mother, and his mother's sister, Mary the wife of Clopas, and Mary Magdalene.

John 19.25

At the heart of the Creeds is the Trinitarian formula of One God, Father, Son and Holy Spirit, a formula which celebrates a God who is all about relationships. Just as we might describe ourselves through how we relate (I am mother to X, son of Y, friend of Z), this concept of identity lies at the heart of the Godhead.

In his life, Jesus deeply interacted not just with the Father but with those around him. He chose a band of friends to work with, he reached out and met those at the fringes of society, and he cried when his friend Lazarus died. However, around the time of his death, some of the interactions showed the very worst of human nature. His close disciple Peter denied that he knew Jesus, Judas betrayed him for money, and he was mocked and beaten by those he came to save.

But his Passion and death also brought out some of the best that human beings are capable of, and he was not alone. Women followed his journey to the cross and wept for him, Simon of Cyrene carried the cross, his mother and the disciple he loved stood by the cross and remained with him.

In the depths of cancer treatment, you are surrounded by a web of love and support from your friends and family, but other relationships may suffer and even cause you pain.

Before I began my treatment I went and officially quit my temporary photocopying job. My diagnosis had been the biggest event of that long summer in the office. My manager cried, and the others didn't know what to say. I confirmed with my PhD supervisor that I needed to delay my studies by a year and he was entirely supportive. Over the next few months, some friends made the long trek north. Two local friends unfailingly met me every week and normality continued in weekly trips to Starbucks and shopping.

I felt like a cancer patient, and I was beginning to look like one too. It is not the hair on your head that matters, but once your eyebrows and eyelashes fall out, it is really obvious. Mum and I went wig shopping, taking our NHS form to the recommended place in a seedy back room of a clothes shop aimed at middle-aged women in the west end of Aberdeen. I wasn't keen, and was even less so when I put one on. Seeing yourself in a wig is like hearing a recording of your voice – it is you, but really not a 'you' that you instantly recognize. A wig was ordered, but never worn. But I dyed my eyebrows back in with some success.

Many friends did not visit, and I was getting used to reading reactions. Often, people would quickly say, 'You look fine,' rather than asking me how I was. I clearly did not look fine.

I felt very confused and disorientated. Having cancer sounds serious, and yet no one was really acting as if this was the case, at least not with me. I went back to Dr M. one day when I was in treatment with a minor complaint. At the end of the appointment he said, 'You know, this is a serious disease. It is OK to be upset about it. And it is OK to talk about your worries.' I instinctively knew that my body was seriously ill, and it was good to hear someone confirm it. There is only so long one can hide in Starbucks and behind a credit card.

The long hours in the haematology department were accompanied by the nursing and support staff. These dedicated and sensitive people met my needs and held my hand through it all, sometimes literally. My nurse Jeff worked with a quiet and complete confidence, never failing to come up with new ways to ease my ever-growing list of symptoms and coaxing my increasingly indignant veins to the surface. He remained with me, and stood by watching, usually with a joke or a new cold compress up his sleeve to help relieve the pain, both physical and existential.

Lonely but held. Alone but surrounded.

Before cancer, people will have known you in a variety of ways: as colleague, church member, friend, child. But once you have cancer, it becomes your chief calling card and the first thing that comes to mind when people think about you or meet you for the first time. You are your disease, at least for a short period, and while friends and family readjust to the new situation, this modification in identity can take time to settle.

One of the hardest identity shifts to make in cancer might be how your appearance is changed by the disease or the treatment. The 'you' on the inside has not changed, but people will see you differently, and strangers will see the balding head or wig before they get a chance to know you. Hair loss is almost synonymous with cancer in the popular understanding and it can be devastating. But it is a sign that the treatment is doing what it should – stopping cell division, not only in your hair follicles but also in the cancerous growth. And it is good to surround yourself with people who don't just see the bald head, but the person underneath. Cope as you can, experiment with hats and scarves if you wish, or don't cover it up at all – rejoice that beauty can include the drawn-in eyebrow and the body that is fighting a disease.

Cancer has a profound impact on our relationships and friendships. Some people simply don't want to engage, and as terrible as this might feel, it is really their issue, not yours. The disciples of Jesus ran away, and didn't want to go near the threat of extreme suffering that Jesus faced. Friends may be afraid to say the wrong thing and upset you, unaware that the isolation this produces is just as upsetting. They may be worried that they cannot cope, for you push the boundary and interject with your simple presence somewhere they don't want to go: the possibility that they too might get ill. It is not easy being the person who makes other people think about death. Pray for them, try not to let it upset you. Look out for signs that people are not able to handle what you are going through, so you are not vulnerable to being let down by them.

Relationships may change for a time: partners become carers, or an adult child returns home for support. Being dependent on others when you are used to self-sufficiency and control may be incredibly tough. We do not like to be vulnerable and ask for help, and our society is the poorer for not valuing the vulnerable.

If there is one theme that encompasses the whole of Jesus, the incarnation of God, it is that God became vulnerable for our salvation. He associated with the dregs of society, he stooped down to wash his disciples' feet and ultimately he handed over his body to the authorities – this was true love. Jesus couldn't carry the cross himself, he thirsted and asked for a drink: he relied on others to meet his needs. He showed that the very best of human nature is utter interdependence and vulnerability.

St Paul himself suffered first with blindness (Acts 9) and then with a 'thorn' (2 Corinthians 12.7), and it is perhaps through his experience of real physical suffering that he was sensitive to this theme in Jesus' witness to God's love. Writing to his community in Corinth about his suffering, Paul says:

> Three times I appealed to the Lord about this, that it would leave me, but he said to me, 'My grace is sufficient for you, for power is made perfect in weakness.' So, I will boast all the more gladly of my weaknesses, so that the power of Christ may dwell in me. Therefore I am content with weaknesses, insults, hardships, persecutions, and calamities for the sake of Christ; for whenever I am weak, then I am strong.
>
> *2 Corinthians 12.8–10*

Many people around you, some near and others further away, will be standing by you at this time. You may have to let them know how to care for you. You may also be worried about how your illness is affecting those that you love. Prayer for your situation and your family may or may not come easily, but God is with you no matter how you feel.

And you are part of a new community now, the cancer community. On the cross, Jesus entrusted his mother to his disciple, and thus began the Church. New green shoots of community can emerge even in the darkest of places. No one ever wants to join the cancer community, but we are part of it nonetheless, and there is opportunity here: a chance to connect with those around you in waiting rooms, on internet forums and in support groups. I have found, years later, that when I talk about my cancer with another member of the cancer community there is an instant bond between us as companions on the journey.

> One of the marvellous things about community is that it enables us to welcome and help people in a way we couldn't as individuals. When we pool our strength and share the work and responsibility, we can welcome many people, even those in deep distress, and perhaps help them find self-confidence and inner healing. *Jean Vanier*[3]

Crucified

And as one from whom others hide their faces
he was despised, and we held him of no account.

Isaiah 53.3b

We are so used to seeing crucifixes that it is easy to overlook the suffering they represent. Crucifixion was an exceptionally cruel method of execution: victims normally took days to die, usually of exhaustion or asphyxiation. Jesus' death was mercifully swifter, perhaps because of the preceding torture.

We now approach the climax of Good Friday as Jesus nears his final moments. Those who loved him hoped desperately that he would climb down from the cross, or that God would save him. But nothing happened. He hung there in pain, crying out, 'My God, my God, why have you forsaken me?'

I cried very little throughout the whole experience. But once, as my Friday treatment was ending, I couldn't bring myself to chat casually about the week ahead or the details of all the pills. I felt desperate, anxious to be out of the clinic, and so I dragged my mum away as quickly as I could, striding out ahead of her across the car park. But I didn't get to the car in time before I was swamped by my own emotions. I let out big wrenching sobs, achingly inconsolable. I just didn't want this to be happening. I was lost in the unfairness, the grief, the physical pain, the loneliness and the anger.

The chemo had begun to burn my arms terribly and neither the hot nor the cold compresses were working any more. I had to arrive at the hospital early and stand with my hands in warm water to coax my scarred veins to the surface. I was very aware that there was a scale of antiemetic drugs, and I did not want to be prescribed the strongest one just in case that too stopped working and I succumbed to continual vomiting. My mouth was full of ulcers. The constipation was unbearable. The chemo dulled my mind, with the result that I was continually forgetting things and getting frustrated.

Each treatment made me ill before I even arrived at the hospital. To begin with I hadn't wanted to be there but in the end I couldn't stand to be there. I couldn't sleep or concentrate; I felt increasingly sick and anxious. On the way to the hospital I would retch and shake – I couldn't physically do this any more, not by myself.

So I started swallowing pills, lovely little blue pills that helped me forget. They dulled the anxiety, and kept me bobbing along on the surface of every day. In this way I ended my chemotherapy, slouching blearily over the finish line, convinced that if it didn't work I wasn't going any further.

In cancer treatment life is destroyed to save life, whether surgically or with radiation or chemicals. The use of chemotherapy, which attacks all cells that divide quickly, means that a balance must be sought between killing the patient and killing the cancer – and it is not always clear which side is winning. The suffering is often worth it, and many more people survive cancer today than in the past. But this is to underplay neither the degree nor the significance of the suffering.

Suffering is a place noted for pain as well as possibility – the possibility of knowledge gained the hard way. But in our journey through the cancer wilderness it is a place that has to be trodden carefully, because it is all too easy to fall victim here to pithy statements and easy slogans. 'What doesn't kill us makes us stronger' is a great song title, but it is not good theology.

What a conscious reflection on suffering might do is lead us away from catchphrases about pain and gain, into really important theological territory; indeed, all theologians, both in the past and today, have considered the problem of suffering – theodicy – to be one of the greatest challenges in human thought. We have a chance then to use our experience of suffering to see what wisdom we can embody as the 'marginal person', the one who stands on the sidelines of life, ill, changed and vulnerable.

What is the suffering entailed by cancer? Is it more than just physical pain? Simone Weil writes about affliction as a state brought about by physical, psychological and social suffering.[4] For her, affliction is different from suffering as it leaves a trace upon one's soul. It might be useful to associate the term affliction with our disease, for cancer involves more than just the body.

First, it may cause psychological pain. This is manifest through the taboo and loneliness of the disease and our fear of physical pain. Cancer can also bring us as humans right up to the edges of our own finitude, plunging us into existential suffering as we trace the outline of our own mortality.

Second, the disease can cause social isolation – friends let us down, and our identity can change in painful and difficult ways. You may be stuck in hospital or unable to move around as you like. Weil writes:

> Affliction is anonymous before all things, it deprives its victims of their personality and makes them into things. It is indifferent; and it is the coldness of this indifference – a metallic coldness – which freezes all those it touches right to the depths of their souls . . . Affliction would not have this power without the element of chance which it contains.[5]

And here is the heart of the matter – 'the element of chance'. We did not choose to get cancer. Cancer happened to us, and we most probably do not know why. This makes the term 'brave' an unsuitable and difficult accolade for the cancer patient. You are brave when you decide to jump into a river to rescue your dog – you didn't have to, you make the decision to risk your life for the animal. People who do that are brave. Cancer is very different and it is unwise to associate the suffering or the sufferer with it.

So, in the suffering of cancer, let's give ourselves a break: we don't have to be brave, cancer is not a question of having great charisma or fortitude. The suffering is deep and diverse and we cope as we can. This disease which is born of chance links us heavily to one question: Why? Why me? Why did I get cancer? It is *the* question which echoes soundlessly around the chemotherapy suite. The same question that was flung from the lips of Jesus as he hung dying on the cross: My God, why did you let this happen?

There are plenty of theological answers. Some are good, some harmful. But if we accept that God created the world in freedom, and that God allows us freedom to live here, then suffering will always be a part of this world. It is the cost of freedom, not the price of bad behaviour. You did not deserve this illness, and you are not to blame for it. The cross shows that there is meaning in the suffering, because God, through the cross, identifies with the suffering world. As Dietrich Bonhoeffer wrote, 'only a suffering god can help'. Because of the cross, through the cross and in the faith of what happened on the cross, we have the firm ground necessary to fling that question to the heavens knowing that Jesus has been here too. And cancer makes it personal, so that the question 'Why?' moves from the abstract to the personal, and we demand in our freedom to know not just 'Why is there suffering?', but 'Why me?'

The old negro spiritual asks, 'Were you there when they crucified the Lord?' I have often sung it on Good Friday amid the desolation of the cross, and before the joy of Easter morning, when I have considered the pain of that death and whether I can ever find an answer to my 'Why?' Something in that old song, and in the old questions, sung in pain and suffering, holds the answer and echoes it back: 'I am with you now in yours.'

To know that it is known – perhaps this is enough for us to bear the suffering. To know that God knows, and is with us. Good Friday is a silent day in the church, no bells or music. And sometimes, though faith remains, the suffering might just be too much for words too. Then we must be OK with silences, and be unafraid of not explaining it away, instead sitting in the dust and ashes of what cancer has done to our lives. To pretend that 'All is well' too early is like booking in a breakdown in the future. Grief papered over, anger hidden away and pain ill expressed will come back to demand that they be dealt with. But know, even in this place of darkness, that you are held by God and those who love you, and that in the silence God hears you cry and catches each tear, loving you and bearing it for you, until you are able to see the light ahead once more.

See, I have inscribed you on the palms of my hands.

Isaiah 49.16a

Death

When Jesus had received the wine, he said, 'It is finished.' Then
he bowed his head and gave up his spirit.   *John 19.30*

Jesus breathed his last and died. It was complete. It was done. He
commended his spirit to God, and breathed his last. Our pilgrimage through cancer will reach a point when the treatment ends,
and the explicit suffering it causes will cease. And there may also
be moments along the way when control is handed over. In these
dreadful but important instants, we give up cancer-free life and
realize that this experience will change us forever.

In between early chemotherapies my parents took me up to
Aviemore in the Highlands of Scotland, a place full for me of childhood memories. The skyline is dominated by ancient mountains and
the air is clear and good. After we arrived at the woodland lodge,
I was lying on the sofa resting as Mum and Dad unpacked the car.

I remember relaxing there, thinking how nice everything was:
I was in one of the most beautiful places in the world, I didn't need
to worry about any responsibilities, we were going to get fish and
chips for dinner, and my last chemo had nearly cleared my body.
I had so much to look forward to in February once my treatment
ended: maybe some travel, back to London to study, and then who
knows? Fall in love? Marriage? Kids?

Suddenly, and for the very first time since I'd struggled to get
off that mountain a few months earlier, I was stuck with the idea
that I might not get better. If the treatment failed, this might not
be done within six months. I might need more treatment. I might
relapse if I went into remission. It might spread undetected into
other parts of my body. I might even die. I could die before I'd
done all the things I wanted.

I knew the survival statistics of my disease, of course, but this
was the moment that it became real, that the possibility of death,
the idea that I might actually perish, entered my consciousness
and became part of my identity. As I lay on that sofa, eyes shut and
giving nothing away, I squeezed back the tears and gave it all to
God. I prayed that God would handle this, for I knew I could not.

A moment's thought, a desperate prayer, and an instant in a dark and dangerous place, when I gave my life to God and started down a new path.

I finished my chemotherapy one grey day in February. I made my escape into the car and home, leaving behind the experience, into one more final recovery in a drug-induced stupor. My physical body, having been infested with and threatened by cancer, had been ravaged by the best of Western medicine in the hunt for the cure. I felt stripped, beaten, alone but surrounded, entering a new region of the wilderness. I may have been bald but I was delighted to be finished.

It is common nowadays to put a picture up on Facebook of your last treatment day, with smiles and thumbs up! And of course, there is so much to celebrate; it is an enormous feat of endurance to get through it all and be able to smile at the end. It is what you have been aiming at for months, and this final day of treatment has been the goal. Rejoice!

But do not be perturbed if you feel a little ambivalent. For there is some way to go through the wilderness yet as we wait to see if the treatment we have endured has done its job. Thankfully, the physical suffering will reduce, but the waiting may be difficult as we wander on, scanning ahead to see if the horizon is brightening.

In church, at the end of the Good Friday service, there is no blessing or dismissal. The vicar will not be standing at the door. The disciples scatter. For them, too, it is over and they wait.

> O Love that wilt not let me go,
> I rest my weary soul in thee;
> I give thee back the life I owe,
> that in thine ocean depths its flow
> may richer, fuller be.

> O Light that followest all my way,
> I yield my flickering torch to thee;
> my heart restores its borrowed ray,
> that in the sunshine's blaze its day
> may brighter, fairer be.

O Joy that seekest me through pain,
I cannot close my heart to thee;
I trace the rainbow through the rain,
and feel the promise is not vain
that morn shall tearless be.

O Cross that liftest up my head,
I dare not ask to fly from thee;
I lay in dust life's glory dead,
and from the ground there blossoms red
life that shall endless be.

4

The vigil

Be strong, and let your heart take courage, all you who
wait for the LORD.

Psalm 31.24

God hidden within me. I find Him by hiding in the silence
in which He is concealed.

Thomas Merton[1]

'The Lord is my portion,' says my soul,
'therefore I will hope in God.'

Lamentations 3.24

Keep watch, dear Lord, with those who wake, or watch,
or weep this night, and give your angels charge over those
who sleep. Tend the sick, give rest to the weary, sustain
the dying, calm the suffering, and pity the distressed; all
for your love's sake, O Christ our Redeemer.

Night Prayer, Daily Variations, Thursday,
Common Worship: Daily Prayer, *p. 346*

Holy Saturday

Then he bought a linen cloth, and taking down the body,
wrapped it in the linen cloth, and laid it in a tomb that had
been hewn out of the rock. He then rolled a stone against
the door of the tomb.   *Mark 15.46*

Immediately after Christ's death, he was taken down from the
cross and placed in the tomb. He lay there dead and the door was

sealed. The disciples fled and in fear they hid away. For them, it had all gone wrong – this was not how it was supposed to end, this was not what they had signed up to. They had believed that he was the Messiah and that there would be a triumphal end to his ministry so that the whole world would believe and their sacrifice would be vindicated. But he was dead and it seemed to be all over. Was it all a waste? Had they been wrong? Could anything good come out of this? The women prepared to tend to the body, and everyone waited and wondered what would happen now.

In our wilderness wanderings, we have come far. The early days of diagnosis seem a world away and our appointment card is now well thumbed and dog-eared. We speak the language of cannula, dosage and dressings, and know the quickest way to the hospital cafeteria and pharmacy. Our bodies have changed and our minds are full of the knowledge of drugs and side effects. We are the bald ones, the ones with no eyebrows, the scarred and the weary ones, on first name terms with the staff as we catch the eye of the newly diagnosed who are so easy to spot in the waiting room. We are the cancer aficionados, the old kids on the block, edging to the exit and hoping for an escape.

The path through treatment may well have been rough and dangerous, but for now it is finished and we pause to see whether the cancer has been rooted out and is in retreat, or whether it is still present in our body. This might be the beginning of a new phase of the journey, or we might be turning back and heading once more into treatment – we wait, and we watch.

Six weeks after I finished chemotherapy, I returned to the hospital, to the machine where it all began. I undressed and got into a thin gown, drank the tracer fluid once more, and lay down in the CT scanner. The room emptied, and the rings clunked and spun around me as I lay prone, silently mapping and discovering the inner workings of my body.

One cold February morning a week later I returned to sit in the now familiar waiting room, in the same plastic seats, sweating and trying not to dwell on the importance of the news I was about to receive. I thought of anything apart from what was about to happen – I aggressively assumed all would be well, I didn't allow myself to have another negative thought or worry.

'Gillian?'

Mr C. shut the door behind me and before he had even sat down, he told me that the news was good. The scan had been clear except for a small residual mass which they thought was probably scar tissue. Another scan would check this out and they didn't want to see me again for a month. It seemed to be over.

I sat upstairs on the bus as it pulled away from the hospital and carried me into town. I called my mum and dad on the phone to tell them the news. Without knowing quite what to do, I went to Starbucks and sat nursing a caramel latte as I waited for the jubilation. The news was undeniably good, I couldn't have asked for more. But I didn't feel that I was out of the woods, not just yet anyway. And so I sat with my coffee, watching the city go about its business as the condensation gathered on the window and marred my view.

Subsequent scans and tests all said the same and I counted myself extremely fortunate to have remained in remission. But in the weeks and months after my treatment ended, while my delighted family watched me take up my 'old life' again, inwardly I struggled. I spent less time at the hospital and had more time to reflect on what had happened to me. There was space now for doubts and questions to emerge and the fear of recurrence kept me awake at night. Why did I get ill? What if it came back?

I did not trust my body any more.

I attempted to return to normal life. I went to London to study and slotted back into my old social life. I took up old hobbies; I went to the pub; I travelled. But I didn't feel like my old self. I had changed and I was struggling to understand who I was post cancer. I kept slipping, falling down into the dark hole that cancer had, uninvited, created in my life. Without control I broke down in unexpected places. I wasn't able to be happy. Each hospital test was preceded by the certainty that I was ill again. I became depressed, and made poor decisions. I had lost all perspective on health – that wasn't a bruise because I had banged into a chair, it was a sign of leukaemia. I didn't get indigestion, I got stomach cancer. Life seemed unstable and I was filled with anxiety, unable to articulate to those around me what was happening and how I was feeling.

I did not know who I was any more.

Where does the cancer journey end? When the treatment finishes, are we simply ejected back into our old lives, either to carry on where we left off, or to face the final journey? For me, when the doctors told me that my lymphoma was in remission, I had assumed that I would simply go 'back to normal'. This was the understandable expectation of those who surrounded me and was indeed what I was looking forward to enjoying. But it is not what happened.

We can make an analogy with the sorting cube toy that we give to babies to play with, challenging them to slot objects through matching holes. I expected to fit back into my old life like the cube which goes through the square hole. Indeed, I tried to go back to my former job, hang out with old friends, do all the things I used to enjoy. But where I'd formerly slotted in quite nicely, after cancer I did not appear to fit any more. And no matter how hard I attempted to shove myself back into the old life, I wasn't going to fit, and it seemed to be hurting me to keep on trying.

The 'happily ever after' version of my cancer is far easier to tell. In the fairytale ending to my story, I went into remission on that February morning and ever since then each sunset has looked more beautiful, each day full of nothing but joy and wonder. In addition, now that I have beaten cancer, I can do anything and no challenge can ever stop me. This is a story that is easy to tell, and it makes people feel good when they hear it.

But while my remission was undeniably wonderful, and life since cancer has at times been blessed and good, the fairytale ending is not the story to which I want to bear witness. For when the doctors told me that they couldn't see cancer in my body any more, I very quickly realized that my journey through the wilderness of cancer was far from over.

Unlike the experience of a broken leg mending or a dodgy appendix being removed, the end of the experience of cancer is far from clear cut. For once the clamour of the waiting room dies down, the frequency of hospital visits is reduced and the medical staff begin to take a step back, there is space to wonder – why did this happen? What does it all mean? And how has it changed me?

When the treatment ceases

Mary Magdalene and the other Mary were there, sitting opposite the tomb.   *Matthew 27.61*

Treatment comes to an end for several reasons: when cancer has been eliminated from the body, when the patient no longer wishes to be treated, or when the doctors no longer believe that treatment can help. The second and third reasons change our direction of travel and the journey becomes the ultimate one, into the love of God. Whatever the reason for the end of cancer treatment, the journey to find meaning and healing continues. Whether it is a journey into God or into a continued life within this mortal coil, we journey on with the risen Christ at our side.

> Even though I walk through the darkest valley,
>   I fear no evil;
> for you are with me;
>   your rod and your staff –
>   they comfort me.
>
> *Psalm 23.4*

If the tests are positive and the treatment has worked, this is a moment to celebrate. It might not feel as you imagined, but it is enormously significant. You have survived a mortal threat, and you have survived the treatment. Your friends and family will be delighted, and you must rightly bask in the positive impact that it has on their lives. They have been standing with you, and their worry for you has been great.

There will come a moment when you suddenly realize that for a minute, an hour or even a day, you haven't thought about your cancer. Like when a motor which has been running in the background is switched off and you notice that the noise has been droning on and masking out other noises and filling your head, so it is when cancer ceases to occupy your every waking minute. Gradually, you will be able to connect with the world outside cancer again. You can breathe more deeply as an enormous weight is lifted from your shoulders.

Many find that remission offers them a gift, a new chance of life, an opportunity to put things into perspective and to order their lives aright. Cancer has reminded them of who they really are, their true purpose, and their remission is going to be spent expressing this. But for many, particularly young people, it comes as a surprise that when treatment ends and remission is tentatively suggested, an immediate return to normality doesn't occur. The focus has rightly been on the moment of remission, and, just as childhood Christmases, so eagerly anticipated, were always disappointing, so too it can be that when remission is reached it is not quite as anticipated.

If this place of waiting and wondering is difficult and confusing, then you have entered the Holy Saturday of your cancer experience, lying between the suffering of the cross and whatever comes next. Understandably, we want to leave the cancer experience behind and get back to living, whatever that might mean. But for many people, the waiting comes first. And so it was for Jesus. He did not move seamlessly from Good Friday to Easter Sunday; his resurrection took time. Jesus waited; the disciples waited; and so must we. We keep vigil in our remission for the resurrection, longing for whatever comes next; we ask what it means to be in remission; and we ask how we might wait well and prepare for the resurrection of our Lord to redeem us and lighten the path that lies ahead.

> Wait for the Lord, whose day is near; wait for the Lord, keep watch, take heart. *Taizé chant*

The remission community

> If mortals die, will they live again? All the days of my service I would wait until my release should come. *Job 14.14*

I recall again the fundraising appeal run by Cancer Research UK with the slogan, 'I shouldn't be here'. The campaign featured people who had survived cancer, pointing out that without the money raised to fund research the treatments that ensured their survival would not have been developed. While this is of course factually correct, it highlights two interrelated points of tension for someone in remission. First, there is the guilt of the survivor – why did you go into remission, while others with the same disease and prognosis did not? It also points to the out-of-sorts nature of survival. We should have died; indeed if we had lived a century ago we would certainly have died. But we survived, so the question becomes – does living become different because of our mere survival thus far?

Cancer survival comes with its own set of issues. The end of treatment and all its unpleasant side effects is to be celebrated, but there is a new set of problems, not least the uncertainty that the initial diagnosis has given us: how can I live well with the sword of Damocles permanently dangling above me? For most people going back to normal is no longer possible after having cancer, because the rational knowledge of our own mortality has become personal.

John Diamond, the British journalist who was treated for throat cancer, describes remission thus:

> Like a lapsed religion it [cancer] may not be at the front of your mind all the time but it is yawning away there at the back, just waiting for those moments when it needs to come forward and remind you that you are part of that community which touched death and touches it still, the community which has seen a doctor look at his boots and say 'I'm sorry, but ...'[2]

Suffering produces change by definition, indeed in Greek the word *patheia* links together the ideas of suffering and change. The degree to which we engage with that change dictates our ability to live fully post cancer. The fairytale ending to cancer stories misses the opportunity of growth and does not allow the experience to have a positive impact on our real identity because it skips to the 'happily-ever-after', missing out the very real suffering that we have experienced on the journey.

Now is the time to allow some of the negative feelings around cancer that you may have suppressed during treatment to come to the surface. Cancer is a genetic illness, with complex origins which are usually hard to pin down. The serendipity of it all creates fear and anger. So go ahead and rail against the way that your body has been changed, the scars that you now carry – Jesus turned over tables in the Temple in the face of injustice, and so you have permission to do so too. Mourn the loss of trust in your own body. Our increased awareness of our own mortality can produce genuine tension that we are ill-advised to ignore.

Some survivors develop post-traumatic stress disorder (PTSD). The trauma might be associated with the diagnosis, the pain of tests or of treatment, the anxiety about test results and stays in hospitals or worry about recurrence. It is normal to worry, but such worries might escalate into signs of PTSD, which include anxiety, flashbacks, feelings of shame or guilt, trouble sleeping and concentrating, feelings of anger or fear or self-destructive behaviour. PTSD can also affect those who have been caring for the person who is ill. Treatments are available, and so if you are at all worried that you might be suffering from the effects of trauma then speak to your doctors and ask for help. Cancer takes us into some dark places of loss and fear, and remission can be an unexpectedly frightening place to dwell.

But just when we need to articulate what has lain in our minds undisturbed while our bodies were treated, support has also gone into retreat, and these fears can become harder to articulate in remission. Our contact with medical professionals is reduced, and family and friends may be trying to move on to less disturbing topics of conversation. It may have been horrendous to stay in hospital and go there so often, but a full appointment card does offer a tangible structure to the days, weeks and months. It may be that we mourn the loss of all the medical attention.

We shouldn't be embarrassed by any of these feelings, because treatment gave us a plan with a clear direction. Our body was probed and marked, we were surrounded by nurses and doctors watching over innumerable blood tests, scans and investigations. In remission the cushions and safety nets are removed and we are left to wander alone for much of the time, wondering what is happening in the body that once demanded such close scrutiny and interest.

In the shadows lurks the possibility that cancer will return, and in the meantime we are left to wait in expectation that our brief remission will come crashing down around us. We are in the halfway house between treatment and whatever lies beyond, and in faith we ask what healing might look like for the members of this, the 'remission community'.

Exploring remission

The word 'remission' comes with a mighty heritage. In the New Testament the meaning of remission is associated with forgiveness of sins. St Augustine writes: 'Forgiveness is the remission of sins. For it is by this that what has been lost, and was found, is saved from being lost again.'[3]

Remission of sins was, from the very early days of the Church, associated with the sacrament of baptism, with the dual purpose of spiritual regeneration and 'forgiveness'. Indeed, in liturgical texts through the ages 'remission' and 'forgiveness' are used interchangeably, the latter finding favour with translators more recently. Although the biblical and liturgical word is not directly linked to remission in a medical setting, the overlap can create a negative and undesired link between sin and ill health. It is worth therefore going further back in time to explore the history of the term.

In the Hebrew Bible, remission from debt was part of the fabric of society. The system of remission is laid out in the book of Deuteronomy: 'Every seventh year you shall grant a remission of debts' (Deuteronomy 15.1).

This practice involved releasing people from monetary debt, and it came with a stark reminder not to be 'hard-hearted or tight fisted' and to emphasize our shared humanity: 'Since there will never cease to be some in need on the earth, I therefore command you, "Open your hand to the poor and needy neighbour in your land"' (Deuteronomy 15.11).

The meaning of remission here is 'letting go' and the idea has roots in the agricultural practice of allowing a field to lie fallow

every seventh year. This was not for reasons of good soil manage-
ment but rather so that the poor might eat, as the field provides
for those in need during its wild year (Exodus 23.10–11). Remission
was a practice that emphasized care for the poor in community,
not so much that they be released from a particular debt but
rather that they be released from slavery to freedom.

Here we might gain some understanding of the word remission
that is pertinent to us, because cancer comes with the potential
for a type of slavery. Slavery to worry about relapse; slavery to being
defined by the cellular multiplication patterns; slavery to our pre-
cancer lives. Hopes for the future become blurred and haunted by these
fears. The present moment is now a place where trauma jostles for
attention with hope, and identity is ruined by ambiguity. If remission
is to be more than just a medical state, we need to seek release, a release
that is at the very least suggested by the etymology of remission itself.

Psychologists and neurologists explain how past experiences
can affect our present emotions through the role of memory and
the unconscious. The French novelist Marcel Proust describes it
poetically in the famous 'Madeleine episode' which occurs in the
first book of *A la recherche du temps perdu*. When the adult protagonist Charles Swann tastes the 'petite Madeleine' dipped in tea
he is immediately transported in a wave of pleasure and emotion
back to a childhood memory of his aunt giving him one of these
little cakes. And this sensory experience opens up in him a hitherto
unexplored part of his identity.

> No sooner had the warm liquid mixed with the crumbs touched
> my palate than a shiver ran through me and I stopped, intent
> upon the extraordinary thing that was happening to me. An
> exquisite pleasure had invaded my senses, something isolated,
> detached, with no suggestion of its origin. And at once the
> vicissitudes of life had become indifferent to me, its disasters
> innocuous, its brevity illusory – this new sensation having
> had the effect, which love has, of filling me with a precious
> essence; or rather this essence was not in me, it was me.[4]

In remission, the memory of what we have been through as
a physical experience can stain life. For me, if I drove past the

hospital I would feel dizzy and nauseous; if I even thought about the meal I was served during my first chemotherapy I would want to vomit. Looking at the back of my own hand would awaken memories of all the times I had sat and stared at it, hoping the nurse would find a vein, or that the needle carrying the cyto-toxic drugs into my veins would not come out so that they burned my flesh. The 'me' had changed, and however much I did not want to accept it, my cancer experience had to become part of my identity in a complicated psychosomatic way.

The bodily experience of cancer is often under-appreciated when it comes to understanding it theologically. Our bodies are integral to how we experience the world and thus they are inherently bound up with our identity. And some changes or experiences our body goes through are so radical that they ask questions of our very identity.

Painful and intrusive manipulations can cause dissociations and feeling of disembodiment for the patient.[5] Perhaps it was a bone marrow core, or less dramatically, the constant needles searching for veins, the radiation beams burning silently, each in its way dissolving the boundaries of our bodies that we hold so dear, if usually unawares. I think I had at least ten CT scans, and numer-ous other tests, but I never once saw any of the images of my own body they produced. Indeed my body became like an alien world, one that was operating, sickening and then healing without refer-ence to my own desires and wishes. Such experiences of illness and medicine can separate the bodily person from the one who lives inside.

When the boundaries of our bodies are trespassed, even if for good reasons, our sense of self begins to dissolve. Cancer can create a dualism, not just of me against 'the alien invaders' but me against myself; there are secrets hidden within me, and inner conflicts I don't know how to control.[6] It is no surprise then that in remission, where we experience such uncertainty about our bodies and the physical treatments that they have gone through, questions of identity come bubbling to the surface.

Cancer is a liminal experience, a place of uncertainty and thresh-old. Normal boundaries are broken down by cancer: patients look different and act differently, they are not part of the normal flow of life, they are unable to enjoy the same mobility as the healthy, perhaps they are unable to work. The disease comes to define the life, and the individual it seems is silenced by the disease and forced to dwell in a shadowy world of treatment and isolation. And the liminality can continue well after treatment has ended. In remission liminality continues: the body might continue to be affected, it might be hard to fit back into your old life, you may still be attached to the hospital through check-ups. You may have ongoing financial issues that occurred because of your illness, fear about your fertility, or you may feel unable to talk to those around you about how you are really coping with your illness.

It is possible, though, that the liminality of both the illness and remission offers opportunity. For liminality suggests separation, and in the Judeo-Christian tradition separation has always pointed to an experience of the divine. In separation from the normal, the everyday, God is somehow easier to recognize. Jesus went into the wilderness to encounter God and to wrestle with his identity as the one chosen by God. The separation from normal life, when our bodies are handed over for treatment and scrutiny, can be therefore also a place of encounter and holiness.

Many books about cancer have a victory storyline with the aforementioned fairytale ending. Others are more negative, suggesting that the experience of cancer is one that can lead us into solidarity with others who suffer, but no further. My experience immediately after cancer suggested that I was still enslaved by the illness, unable to be fully healed and whole. I got stuck for a while in the liminality that cancer had created in my life.

So the question now is, what ending does a remission story have for those who have faith in the resurrection of Christ from the grave? Well, it must reject the fairytale ending because it doesn't take the story of suffering seriously, and it must also reject the negative story that there is no resolution. Instead, the search goes on for liberation from the slavery of cancer and for the healing which, as Rowan Williams puts it, 'frees the person to express what they are made and called to be'.[7]

I consider that the sufferings of this present time are not worth comparing with the glory about to be revealed to us. For the creation waits with eager longing for the revealing of the children of God; for the creation was subjected to futility, not of its own will but by the will of the one who subjected it, in hope that the creation itself will be set free from its bondage to decay and will obtain the freedom of the glory of the children of God.

Romans 8.18–21

Holy waiting

I will wait for the LORD, who is hiding his face from the house of Jacob, and I will hope in him. *Isaiah 8.17*

In the Christian faith waiting is far from a futile or impotent activity, indeed the theme of waiting repeats itself throughout the history of God's people. Sarah and Abraham had to wait until their old age to have a child; the Prophets longed for the intervention of a messiah; Job sat in the dust and ashes of his life while his friends told him to curse God and be done with it; and in both her pregnancy and at the foot of the cross, Mary waited and watched.

It seems that there is something important in waiting, even in the ambiguity of remission. We have some illustrious predecessors to look to as examples of good, faithful waiting and it is our faith that our waiting is hopeful. Now, as in all of Christian living, we look for signs that God is active in our lives, active in the uncertainty in which we continue to live. Indeed, it may be that we don't even quite know what it is we are waiting for. A new identity? Happiness? Knowledge? For sense to emerge out of chaos? An explanation?

The frustration and pain of sitting in the dust and ashes of our remission halfway house is tangible. We don't like waiting, and the pain of waiting is writ large in the impassioned plea of the psalmist: 'How long, O Lord?' (Psalm 13.1). And we are no better at waiting in our own day. We live in a culture of immediacy, expecting news and information at any time of the day or night.

Waiting is not a pleasant experience and we must guard against any false romanticization: biblical waiting is conducted in the desperation of barrenness, in the suffering of the persecuted, through the agony of childbirth. Waiting is tough and we are rightly cautious of placebos or platitudes.

The disciples were not waiting on Holy Saturday in an exalted state of piety. They were afraid and they had been silenced, grieving for what they had lost. They mourned that they had been forced into a narrative that they did not want. This hadn't been how they thought things were going to work out. This wasn't the story that they were supposed to be telling people. Their story had been about a messiah, a saviour. But the ending had changed. It was now failure, defeat and loss and they were silenced in their separation from Christ. Now they felt powerless and afraid, and hid away from the world.

Presumably the resurrection might have happened much sooner. But it didn't. Everyone waited, including the Son of God, and so the conclusion must be that the waiting of Jesus has theological significance. In the time between the death of Christ and his rising we experience silence and darkness, for there is no map through this time – we don't know where Christ went. Holy Saturday is a place that values silence and allows people the opportunity to sit in the dark. It would be false to simply switch on the light – that would only blind those in the dark and further disrupt what is happening in the silence.

The theologian Hans von Balthasar stresses that in his death, Christ has solidarity with the dead. The death of Christ then is not an embarrassing prelude to the resurrection, but a liberating event for all who are estranged, alienated and trapped in suffering. The death of Jesus is more than an expiation of sin, or a product of his incarnation – his death allows us to hope that no matter how much darkness and silence surrounds us, no matter how far we feel from our life, Christ can meet us there. We can watch and wait with real hope, for God has been there too and God acts. For von Balthasar also points to the passivity of Jesus in death – he did not do the rising, it was God who acted. In our remission, our Holy Saturday of waiting, we need not scrape around for the exit, or demand to know our healing as if by sheer effort we might raise ourselves. But, by looking to Jesus' example, we can know that it is God who heals and God who will lead us into the light.

And though this is the faith, and we acknowledge that God will act in us, you might feel inspired to make time and space for yourself and for God in the healing process. You might find solace in waiting, whether in church or a special place of peace and nature. Perhaps go on a retreat to a shrine or organization specially equipped in healing and wholeness. Revisit the people and places that have meaning for you. And ask God in prayer to show you the way.

> For God alone my soul waits in silence;
>> from him comes my salvation.
>>> *Psalm 62.1*

On the cross Jesus cried out 'It is finished.' In the calm and quiet of Holy Saturday, those words echo and grow until they are realized early on Easter morning. We wait and hope in God and scan the horizon for the resurrection dawn to break.

> By the tender mercy of our God,
> the dawn from on high will break upon us,
> to give light to those who sit in darkness and in the
>> shadow of death,
> to guide our feet into the way of peace.
>>> *Luke 1.78–79*

5

Resurrection

————◆•◆•◆————

I will extol you, O LORD, for you have drawn me up,
and did not let my foes rejoice over me.
O LORD my God, I cried to you for help,
and you have healed me . . .
You have turned my mourning into dancing;
you have taken off my sackcloth
and clothed me with joy . . .

Psalm 30.1–2, 11

Early on the first day of the week, while it was still dark,
Mary Magdalene came to the tomb and saw that the stone
had been removed from the tomb.

John 20.1

If the Spirit of him who raised Jesus from the dead dwells
in you, he who raised Christ from the dead will give life to
your mortal bodies also through his Spirit that dwells in you.

Romans 8.11

Joy accompanies the self-affirmation of our essential being
in spite of the inhibitions coming from the accidental
elements in us. Joy is the emotional expression of the
courageous Yes to one's own true being.

Paul Tillich[1]

One of my children's favourite story books is *Tiddler* by Juliet
Donaldson. In it, the eponymous little fish is a dreamer who is
late for school every day because he is thinking up another tall
tale about an imagined adventure. Few of his fishy chums believe
him, but they enjoy the stories, which are told far and wide across

the ocean. One day, Tiddler is 'lost inside his story' and he doesn't see the fishing net that drags him onto a fishing boat and into great danger. Luckily, he is just a 'tiddler', so they throw him back into the ocean, but by this time he is lost in deep and dark waters. Alone and afraid, he realizes that he can only find his way home if he follows his own story back through the sea – everyone has heard of Tiddler, and so if he retraces the stories he will be able to find his way back to someone who has heard them from one of his fishy school friends. And the plan works – he is led home by his very own story.

Although it is an enchanting children's book, the role of story in the rescue of Tiddler points to something that we can relate to as Christians. For our faith is founded on the story of Jesus Christ and, in particular, the story of the resurrection, a narrative that has changed the lives of billions of people. Indeed, the value of story is recognized in clinical and secular settings too, especially in the growing field of narrative medicine which values the stories of patients in their process of diagnosis, treatment and healing.[2]

The resurrection of Jesus from the dead was an event without precedent and with eternal implications. When God raised Jesus from the dead, his mission on earth and all he said and did was ratified; when God raised Jesus from the dead, the Church began and disciples were commissioned to tell the story; when God raised Jesus from the dead, all who believe were given hope and life eternal.

But the disciples were not sitting around and waiting for it to happen – Jesus had died and the disciples were scattered, afraid and seemingly without hope. Their lives had been thrown into complete disarray, and they were lost in the story of Jesus who died on the cross, a story which seemed to have gone so catastrophically wrong. In the face of this personal tragedy for those who knew Jesus, they carried on as they would after any death: the women went early to anoint the body unaware that something earth-shatteringly unexpected was about to happen.

The question of this final chapter of the book is whether a glimmer of that resurrection hope may be found in what comes next for the person with cancer, whether that is more treatment, terminal illness or the experience of remission. While there is no sense that the suffering of the cross, or the resurrection of Christ, can ever be repeated, the question for us is whether the Paschal journey from suffering to resurrection is one that can bring a particular hope and commission. Can an echo of that resurrection be heard by those seeking an end to the liminality brought about by cancer and the terror of recurrence? In what way can a life touched by death and suffering hear and embody the words of peace that the resurrected Christ gave his disciples?

The hope is that we do not have to remain lost in our cancer story, and the faith is that more must be possible than sitting in the doubt and darkness of worry. Indeed, if we are people whose faith is founded on the resurrection of Jesus Christ from the grave, then we must in faith ask God to roll away the stone and let the light shine in on our experience and whatever the future might hold. Indeed, following my own experience and the wisdom gained from the world of narrative medicine, I suggest that our healing might come through the very story that we tell about our journey through the cancer wilderness.

Just as the disciples on the dawn of Easter morning had no idea what was going to happen next, and just as Jesus was not resuscitated but resurrected into something new, so we have the expectation that what comes next will be new and valuable, and possibly even unexpected: 'I am about to do a new thing; now it springs forth, do you not perceive it? I will make a way in the wilderness and rivers in the desert' (Isaiah 43.19).

Shortly after I went into remission, I travelled to Iona with a group from Aberdeen University chaplaincy led by the chaplain Easter Smart. Iona is an island off the west coast of Scotland associated with the country's Christianization by St Columba, who is said to have pitched up there when he was banished from Ireland. In the mid-twentieth century, the Scottish minister George McLeod rebuilt the abbey and established a residential community committed to social justice and worship on that ancient site, often seen as a 'thin place' lying between heaven and earth. And every Wednesday evening they conduct a healing service.

But I did not go. I couldn't bring myself to enter the abbey walls. Instead, I listened through the door to the warm hymns and the gentle liturgy. And then fetched my coat, and went out alone into the dark and stormy night. I stood outside the east end of the abbey, my back against the ancient stone wall, while the gale thumped into the island and whipped up the sea.

What was I doing? Even the mere suggestion of healing had sent me outside into the cold and the dark, such was the fear of exposing my need; the wound was simply too raw and delicate for me to handle such vulnerability. And I was angry at myself for handling it all so badly: I was in remission now, so why did I feel so awful? It was like my identity had been completely scraped away; I did not know who I was any more.

A few years later, in theological college, I was preparing to be ordained a priest. Although I went through counselling following my illness, I decided to spend time looking at my experience theologically and I began by writing my story. I spent time remembering what had happened, and how it had felt. Words tumbled out and emotions I had long ago forgotten bubbled to the surface as I worked my way through the memories of diagnosis and chemotherapy.

When I had finished writing, something very distinctive happened. I felt relief. It was as if I had shoved all the memories into a cupboard and shut the door tight, and the exhausting work of keeping the door shut was now over. I didn't have to bother to put these things back in the cupboard and hide them away now. I printed out two copies and placed them in a blue folder. I suddenly felt very different. I knew where my experience was now. I could touch it and read it, or put it away out of sight. No longer could it creep up on me unawares. No longer would I be sideswiped by it on a dark night and be struck by horror and emptiness. My cancer experience was there in that blue folder, and now I was in control.

After writing my story, I thought it might be interesting to find out what chemotherapy is like for those at the other end of the needle. I emailed my specialist Hodgkin's nurse Jeff and, wondering whether he would remember a patient he'd cared for over eight years earlier, asked if he would be prepared to meet up with me. Within hours I received from him an enthusiastic message. He agreed to meet me and I travelled back to Aberdeen.

Many people were involved in my treatment, but Jeff was the one I spent most time with. He'd explained everything to me, sat with me and helped me through. He'd relieved my symptoms, offered advice and listened to me. He'd waited to see if I would have any adverse effects from the treatment, he knew about the drugs and he knew that what I was experiencing was one of the toughest chemo regimes given to outpatients. He just knew, and meeting him now, years later, meant going back into the experience, as close as I could get without being ill again. I was worried it would be too much, that I might break down when I saw him. I had no idea what was going to happen.

But when we met, lots of things didn't happen – I wasn't sick, I wasn't upset. It didn't destroy me and it wasn't difficult. We talked about treatment and recovery, and about those who didn't survive. We compared notes about what had happened in our lives since we last met.

I rushed home and waited for the tears to start after what was for me a momentous meeting. I had travelled back to my cross, the site of my suffering. Had I been so well protected that I had missed the experience? Had we just been two relative strangers poking around a few shared hours together in the treatment room?

Or had something more profound happened? Jeff had been there and had not left me at my lowest. Of everyone at that time he was as close to experiencing it as anyone, and he had remained there with me. He had not fallen asleep, or changed the topic of conversation, or silenced my fears. He had witnessed. There was no distance in that café in Aberdeen between who I'd been then and who I was now; the fears of the years of remission didn't take over. In the only way possible for me, I met my experience of cancer, peeked into the tomb, but without being overwhelmed. The cancer, my cancer, was not the black monster of fantasy and fear which I imagined it had become. I had forgotten that it had been my everyday experience for a while, and that I had not been

95

alone. Cancer had not ruled over me, it wasn't an alien invading force that had attacked me and that I had defeated. Cancer had been my experience of my own body, a chance occurrence, but mine nonetheless. Something in the meeting had healed the distance between myself and my body. This was new.

Continuity and memory

> Great is this power of memory, exceeding great, O my God – an inner chamber large and boundless! Who has plumbed the depths thereof? *St Augustine*, Confessions *Book 10*

The biblical accounts of the resurrection differ, but this is only to be expected in such a strange and unexpected event. The story had ended with death and darkness; the assumption had been that it was all loss. But now there was a strange new possibility. Life was not going to be the same again and, entirely understandably, it took time for Jesus' friends and disciples to begin to grasp this. On Easter morning, Simon Peter and John ran away from the empty tomb, but Mary stood there weeping. She turned to speak to a man she thought was the gardener, but in the encounter recognized his true identity: 'She turned to him in Hebrew, "Rabbouni!"' (John 20.16).

One of the strangest aspects of the resurrection stories is that Jesus is both recognizable and unrecognizable. Mary, in this scene from John's Gospel, does not identify Jesus until he says her name. And in the story where Jesus appears and walks with his friends on the road to Emmaus (Luke 24.13–35), it is not until they break bread that they recognize that their Lord has been with them the whole time. It is in God's power to make God known, just as it was God who raised Jesus from the dead.

The first point then that we draw from the resurrection stories is that there is some *continuity* with the past for Jesus post resurrection. There is something recognizable in Jesus and in the memory of his life that still connects him to his friends despite what he has been through. Among this recognition and in his appearances there is also an enormous sense of healing. The disciples are forgiven for not believing him and for abandoning him in his time of suffering. Combining the recognition and the reconciliation, for the disciples the past is not forgotten, but is forgiven and healed, and something new is created.

In the case of cancer, healing may not just mean getting better physically; such is the depth of the experience that the reciprocal recovery might be equally significant and possibly life-changing. Part of the restoration process might include healing with regard to some of the many terrible memories and moments that we would rather forget, not only for the person who was ill but for his or her friends and family: real suffering, anger, disappointment and pain are part of the cancer experience. In the light of the resurrection, healing does not mean that the experience is simply forgotten. Healing means more than simple amnesia, and must include, if we take the resurrection seriously, a sense that the past is taken forward into whatever emerges next, whether that is a continued pilgrimage through illness or a journey into remission.

The healing miracles in the Gospels may be read on many levels. For example, the healing of the Gerasene demoniac (Mark 5.1–20) at first reading is an account of someone who is sick getting better. At a second reading we find that it demonstrates the power of Jesus over nature. At a third reading, one that is universal to the healing stories, we see that healing allows reconnection. After he is healed, Jesus says to the man, 'Go home to your friends, and tell them how much the Lord has done for you, and what mercy he has shown you' (Mark 5.19).

The healed man returns to the community and is able to reconnect once again with the world. In many of the Gospel healing stories the theme of reconnection emerges. For healing in cancer, though the illness is not forgotten, the important point is that the period of liminality, the time of wandering in the wilderness, is ended and a reconnection with what went before happens. The affliction of the disease, its social isolation, real pain and psychological stress, is ended and the person with cancer can step out of the shadows. In many ways, there is continuity with the past, with life before the illness, and the same person emerges from the wilderness. But, as the resurrection stories suggest, this is not the full meaning of events. Jesus did not simply return to the earth unchanged, and he had a message that demanded action.

The gift of peace

> When it was evening on that day, the first day of the week, and the doors of the house where the disciples had met were locked for fear of the Jews, Jesus came and stood among them and said, 'Peace be with you.' *John 20.19*

When the disciples see the risen Christ he repeatedly blesses them with *Peace* and tells them not to be afraid, which seems a tall order given that something so extraordinary has just happened.

Rowan Williams holds that health is restored by healing which is more than just a clinical process but one which finds peace between the body and the spirit.[3] He is not advocating a strong dualism between body and spirit, but rather speaking about 'embodied spirits' who seek to understand themselves through their body. This type of healing is about making the connection between self and body, between past and present, between physical reality and future hopes, between created and Creator. Peace is about reconnection.

In the Bible, we are given many examples of the link between the healing of human afflictions and the joy and praise which spring from this hope of a reconnection between God and the universe. In the book of the prophet Isaiah, the people are facing the judgement of God: the land is ravaged, the people are suffering, and there is a huge distance from God. But the future vision is one of hope and healing, of joy and dancing:

> The wilderness and the dry land shall be glad,
> the desert shall rejoice and blossom;
> like the crocus it shall blossom abundantly
> and rejoice with joy and singing.
> *Isaiah 35.1–2*

In the New Testament, the prophetic vision of the future with God is one of healing and reconciliation between earth and heaven, God and humankind. The vision of a new heaven and a new earth is one where there is full connection and peace, with God in the midst of all things: 'he will wipe every tear from their eyes. Death will be no more; mourning and crying and pain will be no more' (Revelation 21.4).

The resurrection gift of peace is from the one who bridges that gap until the day that the vision in Revelation is realized. Jesus speaks peace because he now connects God and creation through his act of death and resurrection and can offer assurance and love to those who follow him.

The resurrection gift of peace is one that the ill and the remission community desperately want to hear. In all the worry about sickness and recurrence, in the broken identities, in fears about the future, the desire is for peace. The temptation is to wish it had not happened, to want things to go back to normal, but this is as unrealistic for us as it was for the disciples wishing that the cross had never happened. The suffering servant now stands and greets us with healing, reconciliation and peace.

In the Greek form peace is ειρενε, which has a spiritualized meaning, and so hints at some of the dualistic problems of early Church doctrine – i.e. peace is sought away from the body, or by rising up out of the trappings of the flesh. The Latin form of peace is *pax*, which has strong connotations of a peace maintained and held militarily: *Pax Romana*, the motto of the Roman army, is a case in point. This might resonate with the peace or ceasefire achieved in cancer by the use of chemical or nuclear weapons of radiotherapy or chemotherapy. The peace that Jesus uttered in the upper room is better expressed in the Hebrew form of peace: *shalom*. This peace, this healing that Jesus announced, implies a sense of well-being, of peace in a community, of the security of being in the right relationship with God. Healing around cancer is about *shalom*.

We remember the words of Luke's Gospel:

By the tender compassion of our God
   the dawn from on high shall break upon us,
to give light to those who dwell in darkness and the shadow
   of death
to guide our feet into the way of peace [*shalom*].

Luke 1.78–79

Can we who are on the cancer journey say instead

> In the love of God with which Jesus suffered as we suffer
> the dawn from on high shall break upon us
> to those being treated for cancer and those lost in remission
> and to guide our scarred bodies into the way of *shalom*.

For peace/*shalom* isn't a ceasefire, or a removal of suffering and strife, or an abandonment of the body with all the illnesses that it can develop. It is about something new: the dawning of life post cancer and the continuation, despite what our bodies have been through, of our status with God: God's beloved creation, in whom God delights.

Raised with scars

Jesus is raised from the dead and appears to his disciples with a message of peace, but he does so bearing the visible scars of his recent suffering: 'Jesus came and stood among them and said, "Peace be with you." After he said this, he showed them his hands and his side' (John 20.20).

There is much discussion about what the resurrected body actually was. There was obviously some continuation: he was recognizable, usually when he wanted to be, and he bore scars connected to his crucifixion. He ate and even cooked a barbecue. But it seemed he could also pass through solid doors. The resurrected Christ was not just a comforting presence, but someone more purposeful and powerful in his activity.

The resurrected, scarred body broke all kinds of taboos, then and now. In the time of the Gospels, there were alternative spiritualities that saw the body as a barrier to the spiritual life, a position nullified by the resurrection. When Christ rose from the dead with a body, the idea that our physical body (along with bodily desire, actions, illness and scars) is any barrier at all to relationship with God was firmly thrown out of our doctrinal handbook. The scars of the risen Christ are important. They affirm the wounded, the survivor; they ratify God's blessing on all kinds of bodies and their experiences: 'In revealing a physically impaired resurrected body, all kinds of taboos are broken. The body that is impaired is ... a new model of wholeness and a symbol of solidarity.'[4]

For the journey of cancer leaves behind scars: both physical and psychological. Either way, they are lasting and, in my experience, are part of what the future looks like too. Like a tree that has branches cut off to allow new growth, it is from the scars of cancer, at first glance so terrible and negative, that new life can emerge.

The American writer Audre Lorde had a mastectomy as part of her breast cancer treatment, and wrote movingly about the political pressure to cover up, and hide away her scars:

> Well, women with breast cancer are warriors, also. I have been to war, and still am ... I refuse to have my scars hidden or trivialized behind lambswool or silicone gel. I refuse to be reduced in my own eyes or in the eyes of others from warrior to mere victim, simply because it might render me a fraction more acceptable or less dangerous to the still complacent, those who believe if you cover up a problem it ceases to exist.[5]

Lorde celebrated her wounds by not hiding them, but allowing them to become part of her new identity. Likewise, the scars of the risen Christ allow freedom for something new to develop directly from the bad experience, when they are reconnected into the present life. When the scarred body is celebrated one is not held back by the suffering it has been through, whether physical, psychological or social. Indeed, the resurrection of Jesus' body with scars deeply ratifies the importance of the body, whatever state it is in. The Church Father Tertullian writes: 'The resurrection hope is thus not an opium of the beyond, but a power of worldly life. The resurrection hope claims paradoxically: *Caro est cardo salutis*.'[6] The Latin may be translated: 'the flesh is the hinge of salvation'.

If Tertullian is right in his interpretation of the resurrection then not only flesh, but everything that happens to our bodies, which are created by God, is part of the bigger picture of life with God. The body is central to Christian life, and to proper resurrection hope: even the cancer-inflicted body, even the scarred remission body: 'But he was pierced for our transgressions, he was crushed for our iniquities; the punishment that brought us peace was on him, and by his wounds we are healed' (Isaiah 53.5, NIV).

The global and the personal

Jesus said to her, 'Mary!'

John 20.16

When God brought Jesus back from the dead, the global event happened through personal encounters, first with Mary and then with the other disciples.[7] In these appearances, from which the resurrection story spread throughout the world, personal stories changed and new identities were created.

The story prior to Jesus' death had been that he was the Messiah and would bring about reconciliation of all people to God. The disciples had very clear ideas of who Jesus should be, and they frequently got into arguments with him over how he should carry out his ministry and the meaning of his position with God. For example, Jesus rebuked Peter in Matthew 16 when he argued with Jesus' teaching that he would undergo great suffering. Once the cross had effectively ruined the story for the disciples, time was needed for a new story to emerge and a new identity to start after the resurrection.

Despite the shock of the cross, the resurrection showed that Jesus was Lord. But more than this, the resurrection of Jesus to Jerusalem made sense of everything before the cross too. For God presumably could have taken him straight to heaven. But God returned him to the creation, and in doing so ratified 'project incarnation'.[8] In retrospect, the stories that Jesus told, his care for the outcast and his preaching about the kingdom of God, made sense from the point of view of the cross. Suddenly, not only was the story of his life worth telling, but the story of the cross was now important. But further, when Jesus was raised and returned to earth, a new idea began: the possibility of healing and reconciliation this side of heaven.

In the creation theology of the Old Testament, God is seen to bring order out of chaos, especially in the Book of Job and the Psalms. As in chaos theory in science, where regular and predictable patterns emerge out of randomness and apparent unpredictability, so God as Creator is understood as doing this work not only in the natural world but also in the chaos of human lives, especially where there is suffering. In the resurrection when Jesus returns to the world, God shows that there is meaning in the world and that order can emerge even out of the darkest chaos.

In cancer and remission, it is not up to us to do the hard work of seeking or demanding an explanation for the cancer. We don't have to carve out a hope or a new identity. God does it: God fashioned order out of chaos, God raised Jesus from the dead, and the resurrected Christ returned to the earth, with all the brokenness and suffering that abounds here, and showed that healing and peace are possible. And he did it in personal encounters and through the utterance of a name.

A new story

Tell me the same old story,
   When you have cause to fear
That this world's empty glory
Is costing me too dear;
   And when the Lord's bright glory
   Is dawning on my soul,
Tell me the old, old story:
   'Christ Jesus makes thee whole.'

A. Katherine Hankey, 1886

The resurrection began the Church, but it happened when the individual vocations of the disciples were given and affirmed. When Jesus spent time with his disciples on the road to Emmaus, he opened their minds to what had happened. In his encounters with Simon Peter, Jesus forgave the past and gave him his new task, to 'Feed my sheep'. Throughout all the resurrection stories, Jesus' words or presence made sense of the past, and gave the disciples the power to tell a very different and very powerful story going into the future.

In cancer, there are different stories that we might want to tell.[9] The first is a restitutive story, which goes something like this:

I have/had cancer, but it has made me stronger and better and everything is fine now. The second is a chaos story: I have/had cancer, I don't know why it happened and it was terrible and I continue not to make sense of it. There is a third option: the quest story. In this narrative, the experience of suffering is taken seriously, but it is not allowed to have the final word. The person adopting the quest narrative neither lets the cancer be ignored nor allows it to overcome: in a quest narrative a new identity is sought in light of the experience. This is the way I have used my experience, and it is the story (to put it rather crudely) that the disciples found themselves involved in when attempting to understand the resurrection. When Jesus appeared from the dead in personal encounters which gave both peace and purpose, the disciples, reacting to what God was doing in their lives, formed a new identity and mission which was to become the basis of the Christian faith. The meaning and the healing was in the story.

Peter argued with Jesus about the suffering he faced, and he abandoned Jesus after his arrest – he had fallen victim to rationalizing Jesus and trying to make sense of the story too early. But after the cross and the resurrection, Peter was able to understand what had happened more clearly, and found a different and altogether more powerful story to tell. After the resurrection Peter grew in understanding, and from that understanding a story emerged, a story which began the Christian Church.

For me, I was able to best understand and reconnect with my story after I had been in remission. There was something deeply powerful in investigating the mystery of what was going on in my cells, in writing my story, in examining others' experience of cancer. Affliction causes powerlessness, and my story gave me back control. Furthermore, something new emerged. It is as if the process of being dragged through cancer, and being scraped and hurt by it, changed me and a new identity post cancer emerged when I took the quest for understanding seriously.

Ultimately, what this is all about, and what the lesson and gift of cancer might be, is the chance to expose the myth that we are truly in control of our own lives. We will all die, none of us know when, and it is harmful to believe that we command this absolute;

in the words of South American bishop Pedro Casaldaliga: 'When you dance with death, you must dance well.' Perhaps when we look honestly at what we have been through and start to be free to 'dance well', then something new and powerful can emerge: a new story and a new identity.

A new mission and identity

> I will not leave you orphaned; I am coming to you. In a little while the world will no longer see me, but you will see me; because I live, you also will live.   *John 14.18–19*

The resurrection of Jesus from the dead is about memory, hope, reconciliation and peace. But it is also about action.

In John 21, after the resurrection, and despite the events of the cross and Easter Day, Simon Peter and some of the other disciples went back to their old lives and started fishing. They were perhaps still 'processing' events, as we might phrase it in our own psychologically aware times. But it was into this place that the resurrected Christ appeared and challenged them to action, commissioning Peter to 'feed my sheep' and 'Follow me'.

What then is the mission for those with the disease and in remission? How can we use our story to bring God's love to others? Rowan Williams develops his definition of healing here, showing that it is not merely personal but contains an imperative to action and vocation: '"Deep calls unto deep" ... If we answer that call, and find our story given back to us, our name and our memory, that story turns the corner into life and promise, and, most importantly, "calling" in the fuller sense.'[10]

Each Christian is called thus: 'you shall love the Lord your God with all your heart, and with all your soul, and with all your mind, and with all your strength ... You shall love your neighbour as yourself' (Mark 12.30–31). It is the little bit at the end that perhaps holds the key for us: 'yourself'. If we are to take the command of God to love seriously, and to begin to work out what our mission of love might be after cancer or in remission, we have to start with ourselves and with loving ourselves, including our scars and fears. These are recognized and loved by God, as we can see in the resurrection of the crucified one, and they are blessed. You are his beloved, whatever the state of your body, and God delights in you.

The next step is using what you have learnt to help others. Whether you like it or not, you are part of the cancer community now and the bond between those touched by the disease is incredibly strong. As Christ was lifted high on the cross for our salvation, and as Moses held up the serpent in the wilderness for the healing of the people of Israel (Numbers 21.7–9), when cancer and the stories of people who are diagnosed with the disease are brought out into the light, healing begins both for those who speak and those who listen. For that is the funny thing about telling your story: when people hear it, it can be healing for them. Sometimes having a moan to a friend can make you feel so much better; being listened to is healing. When we tell our stories of healing and hope, they then become healing to others. Audre Lorde, speaking of the vocation to tell her story, puts it this way: 'It only remained for me to give it voice, to share it for use, that the pain not be wasted.'[11]

For Jesus, in death and suffering there was no communication; communication could only happen once resurrection had happened. For us, cancer has changed who we are but there is power in our story, in both the telling and the listening. Whether the illness is terminal or continues, or if we are in remission, the resurrection has the power to transcend the state of our bodies and the journey that we all must face, and make that journey a pilgrimage of freedom and peace. Like the disciples meeting the risen Christ, there is also a call to action, whereby we have a new mission to tell our stories for healing. And in these stories we may let the love and light of God shine into the darkness of this world for our healing, and for the healing of all those who walk their own pilgrimage through the cancer wilderness.

So if anyone is in Christ, there is a new creation: everything old has passed away; see, everything has become new!

2 Corinthians 5.17

Final words

Just as we are individuals, the significance of our cancer journey and the way it has shaped our identity is entirely unique. But we share one thing: we are beloved by God who has suffered for us, and who conquered death that we might live in freedom.

The pilgrimage through cancer will have undoubtedly been difficult, but we have never journeyed alone and it is in the travelling that we always learn the most. Whether we are still ill, facing the final journey or now in remission, the outcomes of connecting with our own story remain the same: the possibility of freedom and joy, whatever our bodies have been through. The risen Christ walks with us, still encouraging and supporting us through whatever lies ahead.

Cancer remission is tinged with both life and death, and it is something new. Typically in the Bible a change of status is marked by the giving of a new name. Jesus renamed Simon Peter, the rock upon which the Church was to be founded. Saul changed his name to Paul to mark the end of his persecution of Christians and the beginning of his mission to the Gentiles. In the prophetic vision of Revelation, those in the New Heaven were seen with the name of God written on their foreheads.

In baptism, new Christians experience spiritual regeneration and remission of sins. As a symbol of their new status as beloved as God, the sign of the cross is made on their forehead. This is the sign and the seal of their relationship with God, of their new life in communion with God, and the promise of eternal life through Christ. This cross is a symbol of our mortality and a reminder that through the Passion, cross and resurrection of Jesus we are no longer doomed to die, but are guaranteed a new life with God.

The new name for the cancer-remission person is a new identity. It is linked to who we were before the disease randomly started in our body, but it is also informed by what has been learnt along the way, including the healing words of peace, reconnection and action of the risen Christ. We have been remissioned to tell our story and to create communities of healing. The question remains for each of us now: what stories of love will we write with our scarred bodies?

The glory of God is a human being fully alive.

Irenaeus

Notes

A beginning

1 T. Merton, *Thoughts in Solitude* (Baston, MA: Shambhala Publications, 1958).

1 The landscape

1 V. E. Frankl, *Man's Search for Meaning* (New York: Simon & Schuster, 1984).
2 R. Charon, *Narrative Medicine: Honoring the Stories of Illness* (New York: Oxford University Press, 2006), p. 86.
3 <www.genome.gov/10001772/all-about-the-human-genome-project-hgp/>.
4 H. J. Li, S. K. Ray, N. K. Singh, B. Johnston and A. B. Leiter, 'Basic helix-loop-helix transcription factors and enteroendocrine cell differentiation', *Diabetes, Obesity and Metabolism* 13 Suppl 1 (October 2011), 5–12.
5 D. Shemin and D. Rittenberg, 'The life span of the human red blood cell', *Journal of Biological Chemistry* 166: 2 (December 1946), 627–36, at p. 635.
6 R. A. Weinberg, *One Renegade Cell: How Cancer Begins* (New York: Basic Books, 1999).
7 C. Tomasetti and B. Vogelstein, 'Variation in cancer risk among tissues can be explained by the number of stem cell divisions', *Science* 347: 6217 (2 January 2015), 78–81.
8 Cancer Research UK, <http://www.cancerresearchuk.org/>.
9 P. Simon and A. Garfunkel, 'The Sound of Silence', 1964.
10 <https://yougov.co.uk/news/2011/08/15/cancer-britons-most-feared-disease/>.
11 V. Woolf, 'On Being Ill', *New Criterion*, January 1926.
12 *The Guardian*, 14 March 2002.
13 J. Donne, 'Meditation X', *The Complete Poetry and Selected Prose of John Donne*, ed. Charles M. Coffin (New York: Modern Library, 1952), pp. 428–9.
14 The 1971 National Cancer Act, <http://www.cancer.gov/newscenter/1971-nca>.
15 S. Sontag, *Illness as Metaphor* (London: Penguin, 1978), p. 80.

16 L. Armstrong, *It's Not About the Bike* (London: Yellow Jersey Press, 1991), p. 273.

17 J. Diamond, *C: Because Cowards Get Cancer Too* . . . (London: Vermilion, 1998), p. 71.

18 R. T. Penson, L. Schapira, K. J. Daniels, B. A. Chabner, T. J. Lynch Jr, 'Cancer as metaphor', *Oncologist* 9: 6 (2004), 708–16.

19 G. J. Annas, 'Reframing the debate on health care reform by replacing our metaphors', *New England Journal of Medicine* 332 (1999), 744–7.

20 Sontag, *Illness as Metaphor*.

21 I. Kant, *Anthropologie*, 1798.

22 Sontag, *Illness as Metaphor*, p. 23.

23 Sontag, *Illness as Metaphor*, p. 87.

24 *Oxford English Dictionary*, 2nd edn (Oxford: Oxford University Press, 1989).

25 There are a number of exceptions to this, for example extreme ascetic practices in some sects of Christianity.

26 M. Buber, *Ecstatic Confessions*, ed. P. Mendes-Flohr, trans. E. Cameron (San Francisco, CA: Harper and Row, 1985), p. 5.

2 Diagnosis

1 S. Hauerwas, *Naming the Silences: God, Medicine and the Problem of Suffering* (London: T & T Clark International, 2004), p. 62.

2 S. Weil, *Waiting on God* (London: Routledge & Kegan Paul, 1951), p. 72.

3 H. U. von Balthasar, *Mysterium Paschale: The Mystery of Easter* (San Francisco, CA: Ignatius Press, 1990), p. 104.

4 D. Soelle, *Suffering* (Philadelphia, PA: Fortress Press, 1975), p. 76.

5 A. Lorde, *The Cancer Journals* (San Francisco, CA: Aunt Lute Books, 1980), p. 49.

6 L. Lynch, *The C-Word* (London: Arrow Books, 2010), p. 21.

7 R. M. Rilke, 'The Garden of Olives', in M. D. Herter Norton (trans.), *Translations from the Poetry of Rainer Maria Rilke* (New York: W. W. Norton, 1938).

8 Soelle, *Suffering*, p. 86.

3 Treatment

1 H. Camara, *Mach aus mir einen Regenbogen: Mitternächtliche Meditationen* (Zurich: Pendo Verlag, 1981), p. 10; trans. in D. Soelle, *The Silent Cry: Mysticism and Resistance* (Minneapolis, MN: Augsburg Fortress, 2001).

2 Ancient Irish hymn, trans. M. Byrne, 1905, versified by E. Hull, 1912.

3 J. Vanier, *Community and Growth* (London: Darton, Longman & Todd, 1989), p. 271.

4 S. Weil, *Waiting on God* (London: Routledge & Kegan Paul, 1951).
5 Weil, *Waiting on God*, p. 69.

4 The vigil

1 J. Montaldo (ed.), *Entering the Silence: Becoming a Monk and Writer. The Journals of Thomas Merton. Volume 2: 1941–1952* (San Francisco, CA: HarperCollins, 1996), p. 187.
2 J. Diamond, *C: Because Cowards Get Cancer Too...* (London: Vermilion, 1998), p. 8.
3 St Augustine, *On Merit and the Forgiveness of Sins, and the Baptism of Infants*.
4 M. Proust, *A la recherche du temps perdu*, Vol. 1 (London: Vintage, 2002), p. 51.
5 R. Charon, *Narrative Medicine: Honoring the Stories of Illness* (New York: Oxford University Press, 2006).
6 Charon, *Narrative Medicine*, pp. 90–1.
7 R. Williams, 'A theology of health for today', in J. Baxter (ed.), *Wounds that Heal: Theology, Imagination and Health* (London: SPCK, 2007), p. 7.

5 Resurrection

1 P. Tillich, *The Courage to Be* (New Haven, CT: Yale University Press, 2000), p. 14.
2 R. Charon, *Narrative Medicine: Honoring the Stories of Illness* (New York: Oxford University Press, 2006).
3 J. Baxter (ed.), *Wounds that Heal: Theology, Imagination and Health* (London: SPCK, 2007).
4 L. Isherwood, *Introducing Feminist Christologies* (Sheffield, 2001), p. 99.
5 A. Lorde, *The Cancer Journals* (San Francisco, CA: Aunt Lute Books, 1980), p. 60.
6 Tertullian, *De Resurrectione mortuorum* 8.2.
7 There are a number of different accounts in the Gospels about the sequence of events on Easter morning.
8 H. U. von Balthasar, *Mysterium Paschale: The Mystery of Easter* (San Francisco, CA: Ignatius Press, 1990).
9 A. W. Frank, *The Wounded Storyteller: Body, Illness and Ethics* (Chicago, IL: University of Chicago Press, 1997).
10 R. Williams, *Resurrection* (London: Darton, Longman & Todd, 1982), p. 41.
11 Lorde, *Cancer Journals*, p. 14.

Further reading

Cancer science

The following books give good, accessible information on cancer, especially if you want to look in more detail at the science of the disease.

Nessa Carey, *The Epigenetics Revolution* (London: Icon Books, 2012).

Anne Grinyer, *Life after Cancer in Adolescence and Young Adulthood* (Abingdon: Routledge, 2009).

Siddhartha Mukherjee, *The Emperor of all Maladies* (London: Fourth Estate, 2011).

Robert A. Weinberg, *One Renegade Cell: How Cancer Begins* (New York: Basic Books, 1999).

Cancer storytelling

In this book, I have supported the idea that healing is to be found in the telling of our own story. In the same way, engaging with the cancer narratives of others may have an important role to play in our own cancer journey of healing and here are a few that I would recommend for their honesty and wisdom.

Some of these books are incredibly funny, breaking a taboo about laughing and humour when seriously ill – especially Lisa Lynch, whose life with cancer and death from the disease was made into a film. Others are heartbreakingly devastating, in particular the American author Peter de Vries whose book deals with the death of his daughter.

John Diamond, *C: Because Cowards Get Cancer Too . . .* (London: Vermilion, 1998)

Kate Gross, *Late Fragments* (London: HarperCollins, 2014).

Paul Kalanithi, *When Breath Turns to Air* (London: Vintage, 2016).

Audre Lorde, *The Cancer Journals* (San Francisco, CA: Aunt Lute Books, 1980).

Lisa Lynch, *The C-Word* (London: Arrow Books, 2010).

Michael Mayne, *A Year Lost and Found* (London: Darton, Longman & Todd, 2007).

Peter de Vries, *The Blood of the Lamb* (Chicago, IL: University of Chicago Press, 1961).

Theology

Theology is both set in the doctrines of our Church, and is also an incredibly lively place of engagement between the theory of God and how we live our lives. If this book has stirred your interest in engaging with ideas about God and what they mean for dynamic and purposeful living, I would recommend these books as good starters.

Jonathan Baxter (ed.), *Wounds that Heal: Theology, Imagination and Health* (London: SPCK, 2007).

Paul Fiddes, *The Creative Suffering of God* (Oxford: Oxford University Press, 2002).

Paula Gooder, *Body* (London: SPCK, 2016).

Dorothee Soelle, *The Silent Cry: Mysticism and Resistance* (Minneapolis, MN: Augsburg Fortress, 2001).

Dorothee Soelle, *Suffering* (Philadelphia, PA: Fortress Press, 1975).

Paul Tillich, *The Courage to Be* (New Haven, CT: Yale University Press, 2000).

W. H. Vanstone, *The Stature of Waiting* (London: Darton, Longman & Todd, 1982).

Flo's Story

A little story about prayer

After I was widowed, my daughter Jo persuaded me to go to this tea dance in a church hall, a bus ride away from where I live. It was a way to keep fit and meet a few people and really cheered me up, but I still felt empty inside.

One day Dot, the lady who runs the dances, was handing out these little *Prayers on the Move* booklets, so I took one. I hadn't been to church for years and I hadn't prayed for a long time, but reading this little book, by myself, in my own time, the prayers really spoke to me. I realized what had been missing.

The next week, I told Dot that I'd really enjoyed the book and said I thought it would be nice to go to church. Dot said she'd give me a lift. Now I'm going to church every Sunday, I've found my faith again and I'm so happy. That empty feeling inside has gone away and it's all thanks to a little booklet called *Prayers on the Move*.

Inspired by a true story. Names and places have been changed.

Help us to tell more stories like Flo's. Sign up for the newsletter, buy bags, books and travelcard wallets, and make a donation to help more people like Flo find God through a book. www.prayersonthemove.com.